The Sleeping Tiger Revolution

Uncommon Business Sense

Dave Gammon

ISBN: 1500212032
ISBN-13: 978-1500212032

DEDICATION

This book is dedicated to Cindy, my very own Sleeping Tiger.

All of us contain a Sleeping Tiger. It is full of potential, power and possibility, but it remains still and resting. This is more obvious in the world of business than in any other field of human endeavour. When we wake up the Tiger, we unleash creativity, productivity and enthusiasm that will drive massive results, and in return reward us and change the world for the better.

My mission in life is simple.

I kick Tigers.

CONTENTS

Acknowledgments i

A new call to action 1

Foreword...3

A few notes on reading this book 15

Mechanics **17**

Develop a product or service for a market...21

Make customers aware of it and then sell it to them 25

Provide the product or service in a way that makes customers say nice things 45

Sell them more stuff and get them to tell everyone how great you are.....................55

Do all the above in a way that makes a margin.......................................67

Manage all of the cash in and out of the business.................................77

Organization...83

Execution **99**

Intent..103

Focus 113

Action...121

Insight...129

Connection..**137**

Grounding...**153**

Next steps for waking the tiger 177

Appendix 1 - the business scoreboard 181

About the author 189

ACKNOWLEDGMENTS

This book could have never been written without the help of everyone who played a part in my career. Thank you to everyone that worked for me, led me, spent time explaining stuff to me, mentored me and allowed me the honour of mentoring them. Every interaction in the commercial world is a chance for new learning.

Particular thanks to:

Jennifer Manson, Samantha Lynch, Dave Moore and Val Warner for helping me craft this book.

Michael Neill (www.supercoach.com) for continuing to inspire me to find the best path for me.

Dr Joseph Riggio (www.josephriggio.com) for giving me the breakthroughs in thinking to finish this project.

Jim Rohn (www.jimrohn.com) for timeless business and lifestyle wisdom.

A NEW CALL TO ACTION

You are perched on a tiny rock, hurtling through a colossal universe at breakneck speed.

Your rock is the exact distance from the sun to create an environment that can sustain life.

You are made of a tiny amount of matter bound together by enough energy to create 30 atom bombs.

You are a member of the most advanced species yet discovered the vanguard of evolution.

You beat millions of other DNA combinations to be chosen and gifted with life in the genetic lottery.

You are seemingly part of the only species capable of understanding and questioning why and how you got here.

If you were born in the western economic area and are the poorest person here, you are still in the richest 10% of the world's population.

You only use a minute fraction of your capabilities, even when you think you are giving 100%.

ACT LIKE IT!!!

FOREWORD

This is the book I spent most of my life thinking I was too stupid to write. Most of my career I was convinced that at any moment someone was going to burst in to my office and shout, 'We are on to you. How the hell did you think you would get away with fooling us into giving you a big important job like this? Get out!'

Education was an epic fail for me. I left school at sixteen and joined the Civil Service as a Clerical Assistant. Twenty- five years later I found myself as Director of Financial Operations in a major telecommunications company.

On this journey I worked for seven FTSE100 companies, in the retail, telecoms, consumer products, and energy sectors, a telecoms start up, and a global consultancy practice.

Most of my career was spent in corporate audit teams, a function historically regarded as a backwater for people who couldn't cut it as real accountants.

I spent years in this 'backwater' scrutinizing and learning about every aspect of business, debating, facilitating, and arguing with the keenest brains in their fields.

My conclusion after all this time was that I must be missing the point. There was clearly something I didn't understand about business. It was too simple, too logical.

Perhaps there was a party I wasn't invited too; some hidden seam of learning that I needed to access in order to become '**commercially aware**'.

It seemed to me that the only thing that made business difficult was when people's behaviour, lack of understanding or blatant disregard for commercial principles got in the way of common sense. When personal, departmental, or corporate interests clashed, businesses seem to have the uncanny habit of consistently doing the wrong thing.

I moved in to operational management hoping that I would see a different perspective from a position of line responsibility rather than reviewing what others were doing. But, alas, it only confirmed what I had learnt.

It didn't seem to matter what company or sector I went to work for, the pattern was the same. Simple businesses made complicated by politics, power trips, and a complete lack of empathy for other's challenges.

Then it all changed for me. I was involved in a cost cutting exercise based on an arbitrary percentage target, as opposed to a rational leveraged improvement. After reviewing the organization I decided what I could do that would cause the least pain, and went about briefing my teams. I travelled to Darlington to tell a small team of five employees that I would be closing their department. I stuck to my script and kept my stiff upper lip while their tears flowed and the shock hit home for them.

The next morning, back in the comfort and safety of my own office, the phone rang. Before I picked it up I knew something was wrong. It was the manager from Darlington. One of the team members had been found dead at her home that morning.

The whys and wherefores of this sad story are not for this book. But in that moment I knew my days in the corporate world were coming to an end.

I went on to work for another large company, but my heart was not in it from the start. Two years later I left the corporate world and set out on a new adventure.

I gave myself the gift of a six-month break to detox from the corporate world and decide what to do next. As soon as the idea of helping small businesses was presented to me, I knew it would be my next step.

The breadth and depth of my knowledge only became apparent to me when I started working with these small companies. I focused on £1m + turnover companies as I had an endless stream of experience, stories and tools to help them with the challenges of building profit, teams, and systems. I remain in awe of these small business champions. Their willingness to take risks, ask questions, have fun, and learn was truly inspiring.

Yet they still faced the same challenges I had seen in bigger companies. Trying to get their own team members excited and driven was exhausting, inter departmental conflict and resistance to change were all present, just like in a big 'grown up' company.

In a large company you can get by, in the short term at least, with a few tail-dragging employees or the odd bad day. Two unmotivated employees in a twenty strong company is a 10% productivity hit!

I noticed how on 'good' days my clients were full of energy and optimism for their business, and on other days everything was 'turning to rat shit.' It looked like this was driven by events in the business. However, even on weeks when results were good I could turn up to find the owner looking like someone had kicked their pet donkey over.

Obviously it wasn't events driving their attitude. Even as I write this book I have had, in the last few weeks, four conversations with the same client, two of which involved him deciding to walk away from his business and doing something else with his life. The other two conversations were about how things weren't so bad and there was a real breakthrough coming if he just stayed focused.

I began studying mind-set and invested thousands of pounds, and hours of time, working with mentors to understand the workings of people's minds. My own mind provided a good test platform. As my understanding deepened I began to see answers, both in my life and in the lives of my clients. The solutions were simpler than I could imagine.

It took me a year going back over my notes, researching, talking to any director and owner that would listen, as well as reflecting on what had happened to me before all the pieces fell into place.

The path(s) of least resistance

As a river steers a course through the landscape, it bends, twists, speeds up and slows down, widens and narrows, heading for its final destination. To the untrained eye it looks like it is random, and at times, counter intuitive. It is simply following its path of least resistance.

This path is determined by principles that govern how water can move. It will not flow uphill (without a pump), and if the temperature gets too cold it will not flow at all.

Every business has a unique path of least resistance. It may not be the most comfortable, but it is the easiest. This path is governed by commercial principles.

Once an owner, director, or manager finds this path and takes action to move in the right direction, effortless growth and results should follow right? NO!

The complication is that people (customers, investors, stakeholders and employees) all have paths of least resistance towards their goals and dreams too.

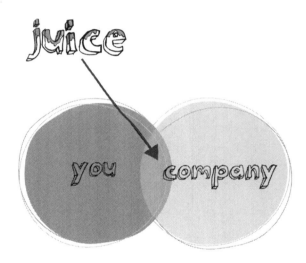

Truly high performance comes when people's own goals and dreams are aligned to those of the business. This explains why small business owners can demonstrate extraordinary drive and willingness to do what it takes.

What keeps companies stuck?

Business is really simple, common sense in fact. Everything you need to know about business can be found in this small book. It is only when you add people that it becomes complicated.

Guesses and trade-offs

'Strategic' decisions are informed guesses about what the business needs to do given the best predictions of the future.

Every aspect of business requires trade-offs. Every company has limited resources. They have to select from unlimited potential courses of action to maximize the return on the investments made.

This should mean that anyone involved in commercial activities will be comfortable with the idea of failure, yet we continue to hang on to the idea that it is a bad thing.

Change

We have run out of ways to describe the pace of change in the world today. Whole industries can disappear in a matter of years and business models that have worked for decades can become obsolete overnight. Managing change is no longer a skill to be mastered; it is a way of life. In this fast moving world we need to operate more than ever from common sense and intuition. Hanging on to traditional models of working is holding companies back.

Overwhelm

People are in a state of overwhelm. Repeated downsizing and restructuring have left fewer brains in companies with the bandwidth to focus and think about the important matters. There are high levels of workplace stress, anxiety, and related illnesses. We are in the worst possible mind-set from which to trust our intuition and use our common sense.

The reaction cycle

So many companies are on a hamster wheel, constantly reacting to changing markets, the demands of customers, and internal problems. Common sense has been buried in the 'one day, I'll get around to it' pile.

Nobody loves you

Society is beginning to put the role of companies under the microscope. No one is enjoying the impact of slowing growth and innovation. It will take new thinking and massive conviction to break this cycle.

Where has the laughter gone?

It used to be fun. An environment of innovation, growth, and connection is a fun place to be. We owe it to employees, customers and suppliers (and to our own blood pressure) to have fun at work.

The effective business person

When coaching small companies the discussions range across all aspects of business (sales, finances, the team, profit margins etc.) We would identify strategies and plans to improve the businesses performance where it was required. But, every now and again, there would be a conversation where I could literally see a light bulb go on. I knew at this point that a permanent change had happened for the client.

> *I ran a six-month program with five businesses focused on sales and marketing. We looked at the sales process and marketing strategies. At the end of the program I asked each one of them what the biggest change in their business was since we started. The answers surprised me, because they were nothing to do with sales or marketing. One of them had improved the relationship with their business partner, another had recruited more team members, and all of them were more positive and confident about their businesses going forward.*

I became curious about how to bypass all the hard work and get people straight to the point of deep change, as experienced by my clients at various points in the coaching program. I realized that unlocking this was the key to helping anyone involved in business.

It became apparent that there were four levers of performance that impacted my clients. The first three are:

1. The extent to which they understood the principles of business and how the main business activities work (**mechanics**)

2. The habitual discipline of creating plans, taking actions and measuring progress (**execution**)

3. The ability to build enduring relationships with their customers, suppliers, employees and colleagues (**connection**)

But there is something else, the fourth driver.

All elite performers in any field (sports, arts, politics, and business) have strong **grounding**. When people are connected to what they do the difference is obvious, in comparison with people who are doing something for money, ego or status.

When you operate from strong grounding you are best placed to trust your intuition and access common sense. Decisions and action become easy.

It's not outside in, it's inside out

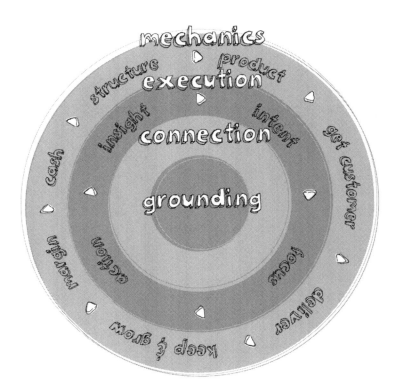

When things are going wrong it looks like the problem is coming from the mechanics of the business, e.g., not making enough sales, declining margin, cash challenges, etc. As a result we try to fix problems at this level. This may work in the short term, but it will only be a question of time before something else goes pop.

The root cause of problems always stem from a lack of grounding and connection in people when decisions are made or actions are taken. If you focus on improving the grounding and connection of the people in the company, the mechanical problems will fix themselves.

Let's take a brief look at each of the four leverage points:

Grounding

When you are at your very best, when ideas come easily, problems get solved and life feels effortless, you are in your best grounding. There are four key questions that I have found useful for helping my clients find their true grounding.

1. Who am I?
2. What do I want?
3. How does the world work?
4. How do I show up?

The more self-aware people become, the more they are able to effortlessly adapt their behaviour to the situations they find themselves in. This is not about getting people to change behaviour, but get them to focus on their true nature.

Pointing people at their grounding may result in some people leaving companies to pursue other vocations. This is a good thing. No-one can be truly effective in a role that is not consistent with their best grounded self.

Connection

The ability to connect with other people is the single most important skill in business, and for that matter, in life. Connecting with someone operates at a deeper level than just words. When people connect at a deep level agreement is reached quicker and there is more commitment to action, as well as a desire to support and help each other.

Spending years as an auditor honed my skills of connecting with people. This was because most people didn't want to talk to me, and when they did, they wanted to share as little information as possible. I learnt to connect with people by being good at three things: shutting up, asking questions, and deeply listening.

Execution

Grounding and connection create ideas and insights that need to be turned into action. I coach all of my clients using four habits of execution.

They are habits for a reason. Habitual behaviour happens without effort or the need for thought. Brushing your teeth does not require huge amounts of concentration or effort. You don't tend to procrastinate or convince yourself that it would be a good thing to do every night. It takes 21 (BSS) repetitions to create a habit, so I don't let people off until they do them without thinking. It is these habits that translate ideas into reality.

The habits are:

- Intent - the ability to 'see' the future outcome required and to build a bridge between 'there' and 'here'.

- Focus - directing the resources you have with intensity onto achieving the future outcome. This includes stopping doing things that are just not important ENOUGH

- Action - doing the things that need to be done.

- Insight - continually measuring progress towards the outcome, and keeping your 'antennas up' for changes happening that may impact your direction.

These are all things that you know damn well are a good idea, but you will always find other activities vying for your time that appear more urgent or important. THEY NEVER ARE!

Mechanics

Business is governed by simple principles. These principles drive activities in a company. I call these the 'mechanics' of business. Without an understanding of these principles and activities you cannot be effective in the world of commerce.

The mechanics of business are:

1. Developing a product or service for a market

2. Making customers aware of it and selling it to them

3. Providing the product or service in a way that makes customers say nice things

4. Selling them more products and getting them to tell everyone how great you are

5. Doing all the above in a way that enables the company to make a margin

6. Managing the cash in and out of the business

7. Building and leveraging the organisation

None of them are difficult to grasp, yet people that work in business do a remarkable job of turning simple into complex. In fact, I maintain that the EVERYday MBA© can be taught to almost anyone in two days.

Grounded, connected, high performing teams working for a company that violates the simple commercial principles in this book will result in COMMERCIAL FAILURE, just as quickly as a miserable team.

Your way or the highway

The context in which every business operates is totally unique to that business. The directors or owners' attitudes and beliefs, their markets, customers, supply chain, products and/or services, teams and systems, create a unique combination.

Copying and implementing everyone else's brilliant ideas; the ones you wrote down in your notebook from leadership development training, MBA, seminars, books, conversations or from the competitor's people you head hunted, is always an option. But have you noticed how the suit never quite fits perfectly?

This book points you in a new direction. The challenges of business are the same. The best-fit solutions are always unique; they never come from someone else's suggested answer.

The game changing business breakthroughs come when people tune into their common sense and convert it into commercial action. You don't need consultants, other people's strategies, or blueprints. You just need to learn what every successful business builder and entrepreneur knows; to trust and follow your gut.

This book is for individuals that are seeking to get the VERY best results from themselves and their teams. It looks in a direction that you have always known is there, but may have chosen to ignore until this moment. Enjoy unlearning everything you thought you knew about being a business Tiger.

"Everything you need is within reach" - Jim Rohn

A FEW NOTES ON READING THIS BOOK

I will occasionally make mention in this book to numbers that are bandied around the world of self-development and business. I use them because they are useful to emphasize a point. My observations of these types of numbers are that:

- The research that supports them seems very difficult to find, or can be subject to multiple interpretations

- They always seem to be a 7 or a multiple of it

- They are averages. There are no average people

To warn you that I have presented a dubious statistic I include a 'BSS' (bullshit statistic) abbreviation next to it. My advice is focus on the point, not the number.

I make NO apology for the simplicity of, and sometimes direct, use of language in this book. I leave the fluff and bullshit to the consultants who will charge you for the privilege.

Detail is interesting, but simplicity is useful.

> *I once wrote a 78-page audit report on a complex technical business system that spanned five different departments of a large company. As a test of whether anyone really absorbed detail, I randomly inserted the word 'cobblers' in one of the findings.*
>
> *Not only did it escape the attention of my own teams QA processes, it was not detected by any of the twenty seven people on the distribution list*

I will emphasize key points and use stories from my own experience, just to highlight how simple people are and business is. Humans have used stories since our early evolution as a way of passing learning down generations.

This book has four simple ideas that help you, and the company, achieve incredible results in life and business.

- You will gain a deeper understanding of yourself (and your own path of least resistance)

- How to connect with other people in a truly impactful way

- The simple habits that translate thought into meaningful action

- The commercial mechanics that underpin any company's success or failure

My sincerest wish is that you find one idea in this book that helps you on your own journey, and helps you avoid many of the mistakes I have made, and seen.

IDEA ONE - MECHANICS

When I was an internal auditor I would often be sent into a subsidiary company and given just few weeks to complete an assessment of how well they were managed. You would think this was nearly impossible having to learn about a whole business and reach a meaningful conclusion in just ten working days!

It wasn't easy, but was not as hard as you would imagine for the simple reason that all businesses operate to the same simple commercial principles and have the same seven basic activities.

- Develop a product or service for a market

- Make customers aware of it, and then sell it to them

- Provide the product or service in a way that makes customers say nice things

- Sell them more products and get them to tell everyone how great you are

- Do all the above in a way that enables the company to make a margin

- Manage all of the cash in and out of the business

- Build and leverage the organization

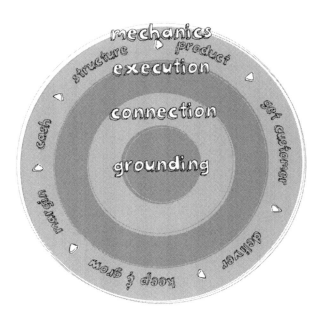

I call these processes and activities business **mechanics**. One you have learnt them they simply need to be applied and kept in mind whenever you are making decisions or taking actions for the company.

If you change companies the mechanics don't change, so in order to understand a business fast, you just need to figure out how they apply them to the new company.

Whatever role you do in your company you will, at some level, impact EVERY ONE of the seven mechanics. Every decision and action taken impacts at least a few of the mechanics.

Each of these mechanics is underpinned by simple principles. A company can only succeed and grow if they operate in a way that is consistent with these principles.

Make Money – the ultimate goal.

PRINCIPLE: Make more in sales than you spend.

The financial goal of a business is to make money, but how much money does it have to make? It should create a sufficient return for the energy, time, and money put into it by the owner and/or investors. It should achieve a satisfactory **RETURN ON INVESTMENT**.

If I had £1m I could choose a range of ways to invest it. I could put it in the bank, back a racehorse, buy property, gold, shares, or setup/buy a business. Each of these options has different risks and rewards. For me to pick a business I would need to believe that the risk and effort was going to be worth the reward or return I would get.

It's the same for a company that is already established. Before investing in more people, equipment, stock, selling space, marketing, or anything else it might need, it will want to be sure that spending that money will generate a return within a reasonable period of time (often called the **PAYBACK PERIOD**). The payback may be achieved through higher sales, lower costs, or improved margin.

The principal measure of business success is how much money the company makes and how much it becomes worth. These are recorded and reported through the financial statements that the company prepares. If you are not familiar with these I have provided an outline in appendix one.

Now forget about money

PRINCIPLE: Focus on customers and product, not profit

Financial targets do not motivate performance from people unless there is a CLEAR / DIRECT and COMPELLING link between their performance and the target. If a company focuses on its products, services and the benefits these bring to customers, profit has an uncanny habit of following closely behind.

I was at a risk management conference when a speaker from a mobile telecommunications operator spoke. As part of his presentation he showed a video outlining their vision for the future. The video showed the day in the life of a woman using mobile technology. At the time of the conference there was no such thing as data services on mobiles, beyond text messaging. It was a deeply moving and inspirational film and I left knowing I wanted to work for that company.

Companies play a bigger role in the world than just to make shareholders money. They shape the lives of the customers they serve, the suppliers who serve them, and the people who choose to come and work for them. They serve society by creating wealth and high quality employment. Companies that focus solely on the maximization of profit will not be successful in recruiting and retaining the most grounded and connected people in a future that shows all the signs of being very different from the past we have lived in. In fact, the only thing we can rely on is that the simple principles on which business success or failure are founded do not change.

MECHANIC ONE - DEVELOP A PRODUCT OR SERVICE FOR A MARKET

What came first, the chicken or the egg?

What came first, the product or the market? It's a chicken and egg dilemma. Some companies create products, and in doing so, create markets. Others watch markets and create products to fit them.

PRINCIPLE - A company must have products or services that meet customer's needs and/or wants.

A business provides products or services (I will now use the word product to mean both), which customers buy. A customer decides whether to buy a product based on how much they want or need it.

It does what it says on the tin

Companies and consumers buy products to resolve a real or perceived need that they have, e.g.:

- I will buy a toilet brush so I don't have to use my hands to clean the toilet

- A company will buy raw materials so that it is able to make products

- Companies buy consultancy to give them strategies for growth or improvement

- My girlfriend will buy a new pair of shoes because fifty pairs is not enough

This basic need is what shapes the product's UTILITY.

Understanding customer's needs is at the core of product design, but there is something else.

Shiny sparkly things

Customers will select a product and pay a premium for it if it has greater 'perceived' value, e.g.:

- I might pay a premium for a toilet brush that matches the colour of my bathroom

- A company might pay more for raw materials that create less waste

- Companies may choose a 'safe option' consultancy firm

- My girlfriend might spend more on shoes that have a Jimmy Choo label on them

This is the extra sparkle a product has. It could be the cache of the brand or something exciting or different about the design.

This is the product's SIGNIFICANCE.

The value of a product is the customer's perception of its combined UTILITY and SIGNIFCANCE.

Nothing lasts forever

Some products feel like they have been around forever, yet all products have a finite lifecycle, consisting of four stages.

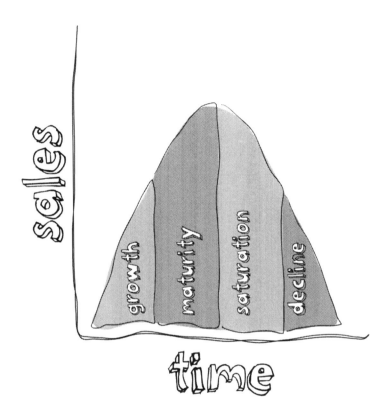

Growth - When a product is launched it is marketed to attract customers. If a product doesn't sell enough to make it profitable, it may be withdrawn.

Maturity - A product reaches a point where it is widely used and sold in its market. This attracts the interest of competitors who will launch their own versions of the product to take some of its market share. The product may require continued marketing or improvements to maintain sales growth.

Saturation - Eventually, if a product keeps selling, it will reach a point where no further growth is possible. This is due to the high percentage of customers who have purchased the product, or a competitor's version of it.

Decline - Sales of all products ultimately decline as alternative choices, changes in customer preferences, or new technologies emerge.

The time period over which the lifecycle of a product happens depends on the product. Heinz Baked Beans have been in the maturity phase for many years (even though many copy products have also entered the market and taken some market share), with only minor recipe and branding modifications along the way. A new mobile phone model can, on the other hand, decline within a year of its launch as a result of the constant launch of new models.

It is for this reason that companies need to continually develop new products and enhance existing ones.

The cooling of the hot tub

> *One of my clients is a hot tub retailer. The hot tub market first started to show significant growth in the UK during the '80s. The growth began to accelerate sharply in the '90s attracting lots of new entrants into the market. We had a discussion, prompted by a slowing of sales, about the point at which the market would reach saturation (when everyone who wants a hot tub has one). After some research with their suppliers and a review of their own business position, we concluded that the point of market saturation was coming. They subsequently made a decision to introduce swimming pools into their product range, a market that has not yet reached maturity in the UK. They continue to sell hot tubs, but now have a new growing source of revenue with which to underpin their continued growth.*

MECHANIC TWO - MAKE CUSTOMERS AWARE OF IT AND THEN SELL IT TO THEM

PRINCIPLE: A company needs to be able to attract sufficient interest from potential customers for its products.

A company needs to make potential customers aware of its product and services. This is called marketing. Its role is to create interest in the product and to get potential customers to express that interest by taking action.

Once a potential customer has expressed interest, the next step is to persuade them to buy your product. This is called sales. The role of sales is to convert the customer's interest into a purchase.

Horse shit aside, what is marketing?

> *Many of my clients are turning over £1-2m. This is typically the size at which a business needs to start taking marketing more seriously. I was discussing the possibility of bringing in a marketing manager with one of my clients when he went into a full meltdown. "I am not bringing in some overpaid, wine drinking, graduate yuppie to waste thousands of pounds in company money to achieve nothing."*

This was an extreme version of a common reaction to any discussion about employing marketing expertise in a business. Never in the field of human endeavour has quite so much cobblers been spouted about a subject, by so few, as in the field of marketing. Marketing is a seemingly complex subject and the confusion is caused by:

- The long list of activities that could fit under the umbrella of marketing

- The lack of a common approach to where marketing fits into the structure of an organization

- The sense of mystery surrounding the black art of marketing

I did an exercise with one of my clients to break marketing down into its component activities so that we could understand what it truly was. We came up with five things:

1. The matching of products to markets

2. Understanding the market, potential customers, and their behaviours and needs

3. Creating campaigns and offers to attract and retain customers

4. Design of branding, copy, advertising, packaging, online presence and printed materials to attract customers

5. Measuring the results and taking corrective action

Suddenly it all seems a little less scary doesn't it?

MARKET

PRINCIPLE: A product needs an ADDRESSABLE TARGET market. Everyone is NOT a market.

Everyone or anyone is NOT a market

There isn't a single product on the planet that everyone would buy. Products are designed to fit a specific group of customers. This group is called the **TARGET MARKET**.

The market needs to be addressable for it to be commercially viable.

This means that there has to be a way to reach the target market in order to generate interest from potential customers.

The target market is made up of customers that fit the profile of people who are most likely to use the company's products. There may be buyers who are not from the target market, but marketing efforts are focused on the target market.

There are countless ways of defining a target market, but they fall into four main groupings:

- Geographic - Grouping by location

- Demographic - Grouping by characteristics, such as age, sex, company turnover, number of employees

- Lifestyle - Groupings based on common interests, social groupings or sectors

- Purchasing - Groupings based on purchasing behaviours and activities

A company can conduct MARKET RESEARCH to find out how many potential customers exist and what their preferences and behaviours are.

PRINCIPLE: The more you define and understand your target market the easier it is to market to them

Carpet vs. precision bombing

During the Second World War, extensive use was made of carpet bombing; a strategy whereby lots of bombs were dropped indiscriminately over an area of ground in the hope that a few of them would hit something important. This is expensive, both in terms of the resources (planes and bombs), and the amount of collateral damage done.

In recent conflicts, the use of precision weapons that are highly targeted has emerged. The idea of these weapons is that they reduce the risk of collateral damage and that they enable warfare to be waged at lower cost.

The more precisely you aim your marketing at specific customers, the better response rate you will get, and the lower your marketing cost per sale generated will be.

One of my clients is a small engineering company comprising two businesses. One of the businesses distributes, designs, and builds solutions with, an aluminium profiling system. This is basically an adult version of Meccano (his description, not mine). The system has been used to build a very wide range of products, including sports shelters, F1 wheel trolleys, airport conveyor systems, office desks, and a wide variety of engineering systems. In discussion with the owner, we concluded that the enquiries they got were so diverse that to try and define a common target market was pointless. Instead, whenever he was asked to build a product that could be sold to other companies, he created specific marketing campaigns to reach out to other customers in that target market. This met with some success and has certainly bought in orders that would have otherwise been lost.

There is no rule that says you can only have ONE target market.

How big is your piece of pie?

It is unlikely that your company is the only one offering products in your chosen target market, and if it is, it won't be forever. The size of a company's piece of the market is called its **MARKET SHARE**, normally expressed as a percentage.

Market share gives an indication of how much a company can grow within its chosen market.

CAMPAIGNS

PRINCIPLE: The cost of acquiring a customer has to be less than the lifetime value of profit that they bring to the company

The purpose of a marketing campaign is to attract potential customers and connect them to the company. There is an important formula that drives the economics of a marketing campaign.

What is a customer worth?

When a new order or sale is won from a new customer, how much is it worth? What does the new customer means to the company over the LIFETIME of the relationship, in terms of:

- their total spend
- the other customers they will refer

This is the **CUSTOMER LIFETIME VALUE**. It is the context for any decision to spend money on marketing. Marketing is an investment, not a cost, and as such, it needs to generate a measurable return.

Buying customers

These days most businesses have to buy customers. They need to spend money just to get potential customers into a conversation with them. This is called an ACQUISITION COST. The amount that a company is prepared to spend to acquire a customer is related to CUSTOMER LIFETIME VALUE as follows

Acquisition Cost < Customer Lifetime Value = Good Business

Acquisition Cost > Customer Lifetime Value = Crap Business

How does this ratio play out in your company?

Extreme acquisition cost

> *The mobile phone industry in the UK provides an interesting, if extreme, example of acquisition cost. When mobile phone technology first become available the handset was given away as part of the contract. This has proved so popular with customers that they still expect it now, years later.*
>
> *If you sign up for a £40 per month 12-month contract, the operator gets £480 of guaranteed revenue. This all seems pretty sweet until you take into account that they give you a handset with a value of at least £250. As if that wasn't bad enough, if you take your contract out through a dealer, they also get to pay commission. In the end the company is left with about £100 of which about 70% was gross profit.*

With no ability to measure how much value is contributed in customers and orders for every marketing pound spent, the company could be flushing money down the toilet.

If I offered you a deal where for every £1 you gave me, I gave you £3 back, how many £1s would you give me? Marketing spend should ALWAYS generate a measurable return on investment.

How to attract potential customers

PRINCIPLE: A company needs marketing channels that attract potential customers to the product

In a target market there will be companies, or consumers, who could use the company's products, but don't. There are principally three reasons for this:

1. They don't know the company exists

2. They use someone else's products

3. They don't know that they need them

The goal of marketing is to CONNECT the two in a way that either gets them to buy something or gets them into a sales process. Good marketing creates the connection.

There are two principal types of marketing to achieve this.

Push marketing directly connects with potential customers and gets them to try the product, or at least open a conversation. Those charming people who phone your home around 6pm are engaged in Push marketing. Telemarketing, door-to-door calling, direct mail outs, and email shots are all examples of PUSH strategies.

The benefit of push marketing is that it can get the customer into a conversation about the product/service. This gives direct feedback on customer interest and can persuade some pioneering customers to try a new product.

The downside of push marketing is that it can create collateral damage for your company, and industry image, if it is perceived as invasive, or disruptive, by customers.

> *I started my coaching business working with a franchise that was broken down into regions. I operated in a region along with ten other coaches. All the coaches were able to market anywhere within the region. The result was carnage. I would go out and visit potential customers and the first thing they would complain about was the volume of calls they got each day from business coaches, many from my franchise! It began to fail as a strategy, which was reflected by the drop in the ratio of calls to appointments made.*

Pull Marketing uses content, or product information, to get the customer to contact the company. Examples of pull marketing are search engine optimized websites, advertisements, press coverage and active referral plans (where customers refer potential customers to the company).

Pull marketing is more comfortable for the customer as they remain in control of the decision to engage. The downside is that it can be an expensive and slow process. It can be difficult to measure and understand specifically how a customer found the company, or what particular marketing gem tipped them towards making contact.

Multiple channels

A marketing channel is a specific route by which potential customers engage with the company. There are four principal channels:

1. Online - customers engage via websites and social media channels

2. Direct - customers engage directly with your sales teams (through showrooms, stores, exhibitions and office, or field based sales people)

3. Indirect - customers engage with another company who are selling your products, such as dealers, wholesalers and online comparison websites

4. Referral - customers engage via existing customers through recommendation

There are few companies that would choose to rely on a single marketing channel, as this can leave them vulnerable if it fails. Most companies have a range of channels and try to ensure that they don't become too reliant on any one of them.

MEASUREMENT - the dirty word

When a client tells me that most of their business comes from recommendation and referral I know what they are really telling me. They don't have a clue where their customers come from.

If a company wants to treat marketing spend as an investment then the 'return on investment' of each campaign has to be tracked. A lot of marketing campaigns do not work. A recent study (2013) of CEO's and senior marketing decision makers concluded that 70% of marketing failed to deliver the expected business results.

Campaign success or failure cannot always be accurately predicted until it is tested in the market place. Tests across a small population can provide a predictor of success before committing to big budget spend.

Advocacy is the ultimate flattery

PRINCIPLE: Every company should aspire to have customers referring other customers as their principle channel for generating new business

As the customer base and product sales grow, the goal of every company should be to harness their customer's goodwill to create recommendations and referrals.

These happen when a happy customer tells other potential customers about the product (in positive terms). The extent to which customers are prepared to recommend the company is the principle indicator of how good its product and customer service is.

Referrals can happen naturally, or can be encouraged, or even rewarded. It is a trade-off to determine the point at which a company actively requests referrals and the design of the referral scheme.

Some customers like to be rewarded for referring customers and others may not be allowed, or want, to accept such rewards. A rule of thumb for a referral campaign is that is should provide some benefit to all three parties, the company, the referred and the referee, even if that benefit is a simple thank you. When in doubt, ask customers.

> *I bought a pair of noise cancelling headphones from Bose shortly after they first became available. I used to fly a lot with work and they were great for making the flight slightly more tolerable. Lots of passengers would ask me about them and I lost count of how many people I let try them. Bose were obviously aware of this behaviour because in the carrying case was a set of Bose business cards to give to people who expressed an interest!*

Understanding which of the company's customers actively refer is important to avoid costly mistakes.

> *Every year I visit my friends who live in the Alps. On one of the local slopes is a brilliant restaurant that is run by an English couple. Every Sunday they do a traditional English roast, and with views over to Mont Blanc, it is about the most perfect place on the planet. My friend takes all of his visitors there and over the years I have recommended it to countless people.*
>
> *On my last visit he returned a main course because it was too dry. The waitress bought a different course and then one of the owners came over to speak to him. What I assumed was to be an apology actually turned into an argument about the meal not being dry. It was very unseemly and a bit embarrassing. He continued to be frosty towards us for the remainder of our visit.*
>
> *I will not go there again, and I guess my friends will think twice. I wonder how much future business they will lose over whether that piece of duck was dry or not?*

KNOW THE RAVING FANS and treat them accordingly. The value of these customers is way beyond what they might spend.

Selling the product

PRINCIPLE: A company needs a process for converting sufficient numbers of potential customers into sales

"Until you reach a million it is ALL about sales" - Vern Harnish

Selling is the single most important mechanic in ANY business. Without sales there is no company.

Selling should focus on building deep connections with potential customers. People who develop good sales skills are invaluable in any market place. Anyone can become great at the game of selling. The only thing that stops them is beliefs about what selling is, and what it involves.

> *When I was a child I vividly remember my mother making me hide behind the sofa when the Insurance salesman came to call. I was under threat of death. Having tried the door I remember him coming around the front of the house and looking through the window. It scared the life out of me.*

I run an exercise when training non-sales people in sales. I ask them to shout out the first word that comes into their mind when I say *salesman*. You can imagine the types of response, which over the years have included bullshit, pushy, money driven, greedy, ruthless, the list goes on. If this is the level of thinking that people bring into conversations about sales, is it any wonder that the profession struggles to attract, and keep, good people?

The sales myth

The most enduring and damaging myth for the sales profession is that in order to be good at sales, you have to somehow coerce and force customers to buy.

I've got bad news if this is what you do. The world of the 'foot in the door' and 'not leaving without a cheque' salesperson is LONG gone.

Potential customers can smell sales pitches a mile off and are far less likely to buy from someone who adopts these tactics.

Selling has become less about persuasion and 'forcing customers to sign' and more about building relationships and helping customers. Old school practices still exist, but they are rapidly heading for extinction.

Knowledge is power

The change in the role of salespeople has been driven by the ever-increasing range of products, methods of purchase, and most importantly, the customer's ability to access all of the information they need to choose a product, without leaving their chair.

Social media, online forums and websites now enable customers to research choices and also to gather the views of other customers. The potential customer can have as much, if not more, market knowledge than the salesperson.

The role of sales is now to help the customer make an informed decision so that they buy the best product, and to build a relationship in order to make future sales.

Sell the wrong solution for a customer and it will be the last order you get from them.

A sales conversation could be anything from a thirty second exchange at a cigarette kiosk where the customer knows the exact brand and quantity they want, to replacing a fleet of airliners requiring extensive sales activity over many years.

Sales is simply the process of converting potential customers into real customers.

The sales funnel

"Samson killed a thousand men with the jaw bone of an ass. That many sales are killed every day with the same weapon." Unknown

I worked for a consultancy practice. The partner that I reported to had a very simple way of measuring the progress of targeting companies we wanted to work with. On the wall of the office was a simple funnel diagram like this one.

You can see that the key steps in the sales process are laid out and the diagram came with one rule. Every target had to move one step down the funnel each month, or we would be asked why.

Customers have different ways of making buying decisions. It is important to understand who is making the decision and on what basis. Good salespeople guide customers through the company's process. This gives them the best opportunity to build trust and present their products well.

There are four things that need to happen for a customer to buy a product from a particular company. The sales funnel needs to ensure that these things happen in a way that:

- maximizes the chances of the customer buying

- ensures the value of the sale is as large as possible

- sets up a long term relationship with the customer

- is consistent

The customer needs the following:

1. BELIEF in the product and the company. Customers will buy from people that they like and trust.

2. An OPPORTUNITY TO SPEAK and to explain their needs. Failure to sell comes from not understanding a customer's challenges and needs.

3. To UNDERSTAND THE BENEFITS of the product in relation to their needs. Customers are not interested in a detailed explanation of the product's features. They want to know how the product will benefit them and solve their challenges.

4. A CHANCE TO BUY. 70% (BSS) of salespeople do not ask the customer if they want to buy the product. Just asking for the sale has changed the fortunes of more of my clients than any other idea. Asking for the sale is important because of the LAW of DIMINISHING INTENT. If the first three steps have been well managed, the customer will be excited and ready to make a decision. If they are allowed to 'go away and think about it', their interest levels exponentially drops.

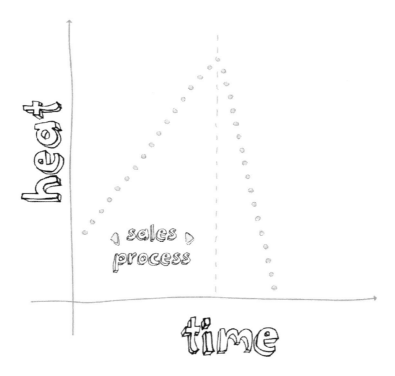

The skills needed to be a great salesperson are no different to the skills to be effective in any business context. They are covered in the sections to follow on execution, connection, and grounding.

Small details can be the difference between a customer buying from a company or not. Every document, script, and element of the sales process should be designed with the customer in mind. For a significant purchase a customer needs seven (BSS) separate touches (brochure, email, conversations, etc.) in the sale process.

One of my clients built high quality bespoke swimming pools with a typical sale value above £70k. On one occasion we looked over the proposal document that was sent to a potential customer. It was created on a word processor and sent to the client. It contained a lot of technical information and of course, the pricing for the pool. The following week I took a copy of a car brochure to them. The price of the model in the brochure ranged from £20-45k, significantly less than one of their pools. My client understood the point straight away and set about re-designing his proposals to better reflect the value of the sale.

Having a sales process that is built around these four conditions for buying maximizes the possibility that the sale will be made and a relationship will prosper.

The money on the table

The famous McDonalds line, "do you want fries with that?" could be one of the most important cross selling strategies ever deployed, adding millions of pounds to their revenue line every day.

What are the fries in your company? An important goal in the sales process is to explore options with the customer and to not leave money on the table. The customer should be aware of the different options (and their pros and cons), and the additional products that the company sells.

Horses for courses

There are four different types of salesperson. The type a company needs for its products depends on two things:

- Product complexity - how hard is the product to understand and how customizable is it

- Customer need awareness - the extent to which the customer understands what they need

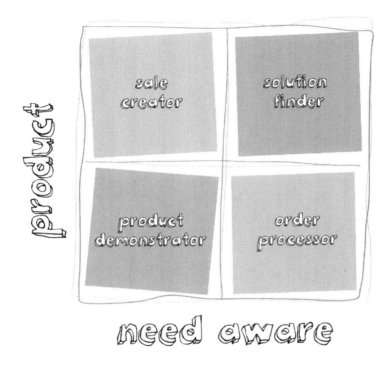

Order Processor - When the customer knows what they want and it's a simple product to understand, e.g. a beef burger. The role of the salesperson is to take the order details and offer any additional products.

Product demonstrator - When the customer does not have an awareness of their need, a demonstration of the product can raise the customers 'need' awareness and prompt a purchase.

> *I recently attended the Ideal Home show, the spiritual home of Product Demonstrator salespeople. Many of the products just look like a crap piece of plastic until the demonstrator deftly, and with seemingly no effort, peels an orange or shapes an onion like a lotus flower. The best demonstrators have people virtually throwing money at them.*

Solution Finder – Solution finders are used when the customer knows they have to solve a problem, but are unsure of how, or what, they need to do. The salesperson asks good questions, listens, and then shows the customer how their product can solve the problem.

Sale Creator - The pinnacle of sales skill is to be able to create a sale from nothing. In other words, to create a need that the customer was not aware of and to design a solution that creates value for them.

> *As a business coach I always said that my biggest competitor was, 'do nothing'. Many of my meetings were with business owners who had little more than a mild curiosity for what I did. The onus was on me to take them on a journey of discovery to help them see that the results they were getting could be much better, and then to explain how spending time, and cash, with me, could help them achieve that.*

A company should make sure it has the right type of salespeople for its products.

Audi vs. McDonalds

> *A few years ago I was in the market for a new car. I decided I was going to buy an Audi and had pretty much made my mind up about the model, but was open to other options. By remarkable good fortune my local showroom had an ex-demo of the very model I wanted, so I paid them a visit. The salesperson took me out for a test drive before taking me through the purchasing options. I decided to have lunch while I thought the purchase over, so I went into town and paid a visit to McDonalds.*

> *I hadn't eaten in McDonalds for a number of years and was surprised, and even confused, at the variety on the menu. The server asked me for my order and I said I wasn't sure. She asked me what I used to like at McDonalds and how important was healthy eating to me, before I opted for my old childhood favourite meal. As I sat having lunch it occurred to me that she had just asked me more questions in relation to a £5.00 purchase than the car salesman had asked me for a*

£30,000 purchase.

I returned to the dealership and, after some price haggling, I ended up buying the ex-demo. His manager would probably be thinking it was a job well done. NO. It is lazy selling epitomized. He just took the path of least resistance, which was to process the order for whatever I said I wanted. He showed no interest in me, or what I was looking for in a car.

Within six months I wished I had bought a convertible (my previous two cars had been convertibles). With just a few questions and a genuine interest in me, the salesman could have moved me up the value chain and established a relationship with me for future car purchases, and perhaps I would have recommended him to friends as well.

Conversion rate

PRINCIPLE: A company needs to convert potential customers into sales at a sufficient rate

The main measure of a salespersons success is the rate at which they convert potential sales into actual sales. This is their **CONVERSION RATE**. It is most often expressed as a percentage (if a salesperson sits ten appointments and three of them become customers, his conversion rate is 3 in 10 or 30%).

The measurement of conversion rate provides insight into the performance of salespeople, and highlights areas where the sales process may need to be improved.

The handover

In many companies upon sale completion, there needs to be a handover to whoever is going to prepare and deliver the product. This is a common failure point.

How it looks to the Delivery team

Once the customer agrees to buy, the sales people disappear over the horizon 'high fiving' each other and guzzling champagne while we get left to figure out what we are delivering.

How it looks to the Sales team

All of our time is taken up, time which we should be using to get the next sale, dealing with queries and questions from the delivery people, who can't seem to get anything right.

PRINCIPLE - Just because you have won the order does not mean that you have won the customer.

Salespeople SELL, Delivery people DELIVER. There must ALWAYS be an effective handover between the two.

> *One of my clients was encountering problems with the handover between the salespeople and the account managers who were responsible for delivering work to the customer. As a result, salespeople were reluctant to hand the customer over believing that the account managers would make a mess of things. Conversely, the account managers were stressed and anxious because they were not being given all of the information they needed in order to deliver for the customer.*
>
> *The result was internal chaos, errors and lots of time wasting. From a customer's perspective, there were examples of multiple requests for information, confusion about who they were supposed to deal with and the occasional (but miraculously rare) delivery error.*
>
> *As an interim fix, the business developed a simple handover checklist to be signed off by the salesperson and the account manager. This had the effect of forcing the real issues out onto the table. Ultimately, the problem will be solved by developing a 'clean order' process whereby the salesperson can only book an order in when all of the relevant information has been provided.*

MECHANIC THREE - PROVIDE THE PRODUCT OR SERVICE IN A WAY THAT MAKES CUSTOMERS SAY NICE THINGS

PRINCIPLE - The only acceptable product and standard of service is the one the customer expected.

The delivery of the product to a customer can be as simple as placing it in a bag and wishing them a good afternoon, or as complex as a project, spanning many years, with regular customer updates and interactions.

The principles of delivery are the same regardless.

A customer's opinion of whether the company did a good job of delivering the product is the only one that matters. What the team thinks does not count. It will not influence whether the customer comes back or refers the company to others.

The customer's expectation is set long before they decide to buy. The expectations come from branding, advertising, the look and feel of your product, what other customers say, and what the salesperson told them.

The customer's expectation may not be a 'world class' service company. When I shop at Lidl I expect there to be longer queues, that not everything I want will be in stock, and that I won't get that warm Waitrose feeling. My EXPECTATION of Lidl is that it is cheap, not that I am going to feel like a god amongst men as I peruse the aisles.

What customers want is a **CONSISTENT** experience; consistent with what they expected, and consistent every time they buy.

PRINCIPLE - a company needs a way to deliver its product or service in a way that fits their customer's needs, CONSISTENTLY

In my early career, I worked for a major food retailer. I was lucky to be taken out on a store visit with one of the very senior directors. This chain had about six hundred stores in the U.K., and he was responsible for a hundred of them.

He was a very serious but engaging guy, an old school retailer. As we went around the store, I noticed him picking up products and looking at packaging, running his finger along the shelf underneath the product, looking at the floor, going up and checking staff uniforms.

I was surprised, so I asked him a question. "Look, you're a senior director; you must be very busy, with a lot on your mind. Why are you focusing on this level of detail in one store?"

He looked at me and said, "Son, retail is detail. If I can't trust my store manager to get these little things right how can I trust him with the big decisions?"

The difference between consistency and inconsistency is the attention to details. Even if customers don't consciously notice the little things, they will still sub-consciously register.

One of my clients had a customer who he regularly provided a standard product to. The customer used to buy about four or five of the same product every month. The product was packed, shipped, and the customer would assemble the product when it arrived.

There had been a couple of grumbles from the customer. Sometimes when they opened the box the parts had moved about, and although the product wasn't damaged, it was quite difficult to empty the box and make sure they had all the components. He could have bought the product from alternative suppliers and my client didn't want to lose him.

My client solved the problem by designing specific packaging at a minimal extra cost. Now when the customer opens the box, the components look like a new set of Meccano, all laid out as it should be. That small change transformed that customer's experience and ensured their loyalty.

By focusing on the small details, a company removes the risk of not meeting their customer's expectations.

It's not difficult. If everyone in the company went about doing their job as if a customer was following them and watching their every move, it would always go smoothly.

PRINCIPLE - The customer wants the benefits that come with having the right product, to receive it when you said they would and to be kept aware of what is going on.

All a company has to do is:

- Have the product the customer wants, when they want it
- Commit to, and meet, an acceptable timescale for when the customer will receive the product
- Send the right product to them
- Ensure the product is of the quality the customer was expecting
- Keep the customer aware of what is happening
- Be helpful when the customer needs help

To achieve this requires two things, good people, and good process. One or the other won't do.

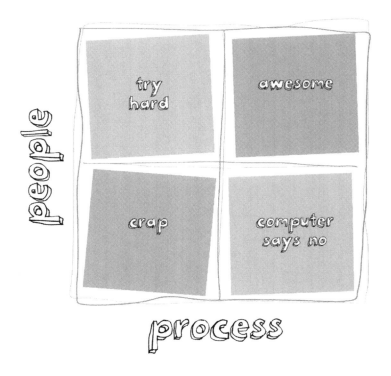

Awesome - The right attitude/training combined with good processes and policies will ensure the customer is consistently well treated.

Try Hard - Good people with weak process will result in customers not getting what they want, but they will be full of praise for the people trying to help them.

Computer says no - Poorly trained people with good process leave the customer frustrated. When have the words 'our policy is....' ever turned out well for a customer?

Crap - Poorly trained and motivated people combined with poor process is what leaves customers frustrated, angry and determined not to use the company again.

PRINCIPLE - A company has to understand the trade-off between product quality, customer service, and margin to experience commercial success

Good product availability and quality, coupled with high levels of customer support and communication costs money. This is a trade-off that every company has to make.

I was sent a picture of a shop sign from the United States which read as follows:

We do three grades of service. You can pick any two.

CHEAP
FAST
GOOD

You can have it Cheap and Fast, but it won't be Good

You can have it Good and Cheap, but it won't be Fast

You can have it Fast and Good, but it won't be Cheap

Squaring the triangle

There is a three-way trade-off in business between the product quality, customer service and the profit margin. One cannot change without impacting the others.

When you add up the angles of the three sides of a triangle, they will always add up to 180 degrees. A triangle with equal sides is called an Isosceles triangle. All of the angles are 60 degrees. Imagine this is your company when it is operating normally. It looks like this.

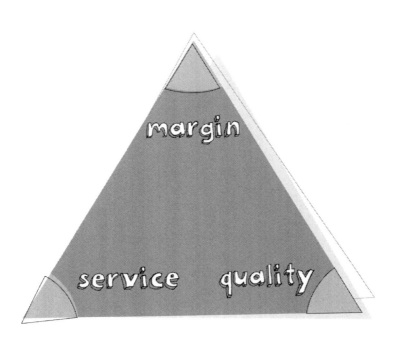

Now imagine a customer wants a product manufactured quicker than usual. This requires re-scheduling production, overtime and a less efficient manufacturing process. As a result the triangle gets skewed:

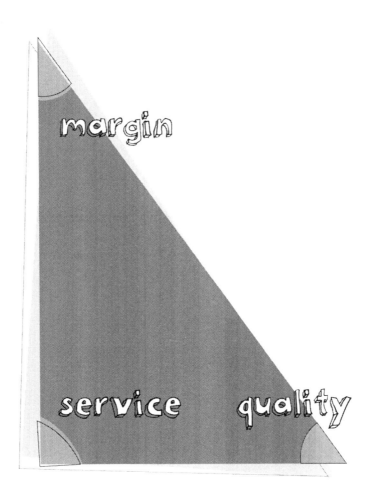

In another scenario, a company cuts its customer service investment. This will impact the triangle as below:

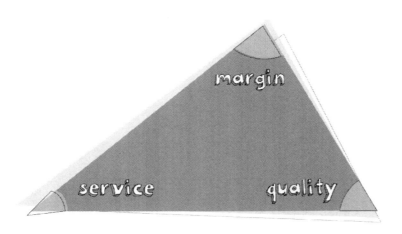

The goal is to keep balance in the triangle. If the customer demands cheap, fast and good something has to give unless a leveraged solution can be found (where a change reduces the cost of product quality or customer service).

Touching the customer
The process by which a company delivers its product to a customer will be unique. I get my clients to create a flowchart or checklist of this process. Then I make sure that everyone in the business understands how it works, because:

- Fulfilling a customer order tends to impact most departments in a company. Everyone needs to see how they fit in and how they impact each other and the customer

- A process creates consistency. Consistency is king when it comes to customer experience

- Problem areas can be identified in the process where bottlenecks happen or errors occur, and improvements can be made

Particular focus should be given to customer touch points. These are the 'moments of truth' in the process, the steps that the customer sees or is involved in.

The inevitable visit of Mr Cock-up

Delivering a product to customers involves people. This means that from time to time, things will go wrong. Cock-ups and the subsequent distress for the customer are inevitable.

PRINCIPLE: When you receive a complaint, the goal is to create a raving fan.

How you handle a complaint matters a lot. Research suggests that people tell, on average, eight (BSS) other people about a problem they had with a company.

FIX IT FOR THE CUSTOMER - then do something astounding for them.

FIGURE OUT WHAT HAPPENED INTERNALLY - the post-mortem happens once the customer is happy - NOT BEFORE.

FIX THE PROCESS to prevent recurrence.

A complaint is a GIFT. It is an insight into how improvements can be made to the company. A company cannot buy this insight; only earn it by cocking up occasionally.

> *One of my clients owns a restaurant. I remember one particular occasion where a customer, in a party of four, had claimed that a meal had made them ill.*
>
> *The owner thoroughly investigated the cooking and preparation of the food and found no evidence to suggest that there had been a problem. Irrespective of that, I asked my client "how have you responded to the customer?"*
>
> *The owner had immediately invited the customer and their guests back for a complimentary meal. His awareness of the idea of turning a complaining customer into an advocate worked. The customer went from being very unhappy to a regular visitor to the restaurant. WIN!*

Satisfaction means nothing

Is customer satisfaction really the best a company should aspire to? Should a restaurant be happy with customers who say, "We had a satisfactory meal. Thank you."

The only measure of real value to a company is whether customers would ACTIVELY recommend them to their friends instead of their enemies.

Asking customers for feedback, whilst interesting, frequently misses the mark. Here are two questions to ask customers that will give genuine improvement insight;

1. What one thing could we do to make your experience even better next time?
2. What is the most frustrating thing you find when dealing with our industry?

When a company has the balls to ask, and act on the answers to these questions, they can make big steps forward and separate themselves from the pack.

MECHANIC FOUR - SELL THEM MORE STUFF AND GET THEM TO TELL EVERYONE HOW GREAT YOU ARE

Tesco are arguably one of the most successful companies at understanding complex customer spending patterns. Their super successful Clubcard enables them to gather detailed information on what their customers spend, what they buy, and how often they shop. Although launched as a scheme to reward the loyalty of their customers, the real juice in the scheme is the information and insights they have gleaned about customer behaviour.

Few companies have a really clear understanding of sales by customer (a look at the invoicing system can be a starting point). How much your customers spend, what they are buying and how often they are buying, are important questions.

PRINCIPLE: It is easier to sell more products to an existing customer than it is to sell a product to a new one

It costs, on average, seven (BSS) times more to attract and win a new customer than it does to sell the same value to an existing one. This is a dangerous average, but the principle is sound. Once a company has won an order the goal is to keep the customer buying.

The customer target

Many company directors and owners that I meet claim that increasing revenue is a priority. This is regularly followed with the phrase 'we need more customers'. The obsession with new customers is based on a misunderstanding of the fastest way to grow revenue. I developed the revenue target to illustrate this.

This is a tool to create rapid revenue growth. It operates from the inside out. You gather data, then design and target campaigns and actions in the following order:

Plan 1: Existing customers - what additional products and services can be sold to existing customers.

Plan 2: Old customers - how many customers have left, why did they go, and what can be done to get them spending again.

Plan 3: Old potential customers - What customers went through the sales process before and didn't buy and how can the conversation be opened up with them again.

Plan 4: New potential customers - How to target new potential customers in the target market.

Some of my clients have found it helpful to further sub-divide each of the rings in the target, e.g., to separate old customers into age bands, less than six months, over a year, etc.

If the company has invested time and effort in building trust with customers, extracting more revenue from them is the easiest place to start.

When is a customer not a customer?

PRINCIPLE: A customer who buys from a company once is not a customer. They become a customer when they buy several times. A customer is a relationship not just a sale.

> *One of my clients did some analysis of customers who purchased from their online shop. They found that over 70% of them only purchased from the website once. They were horrified but I was excited. What an opportunity to grow revenue!*

After the first time purchase, the company should focus on getting the customer to buy again. It is then possible to build a relationship with the customer.

It is necessary to capture information about them in order to grow this relationship. The amount of times a company communicates with a customer is a difficult balance to strike, and there are already signs that it is becoming increasingly difficult to get customers to part with contact details.

> *One of my clients sells point of sale products to retail stores and product manufacturers. They set up a website with an online store and began to win sales through this channel. Most of the customers only bought from the site once. To overcome this, they started to send a letter after the product was dispatched with a discount voucher for their next purchase, and a copy of their product catalogue. In addition, they scheduled a call with the customer to make sure they were satisfied with the product they received, and to introduce the company.*
>
> *This had the effect of beginning to build a relationship with the customer and getting them to purchase other products.*

Deepening the relationship

Over a longer period of time a company can build a profile of what customers are spending and when. Some companies can start to accurately predict their customers spending patterns and behaviour. This means they can ensure availability and advise the customer on new products, or changes that affect them. This further deepens the relationship with the customer.

> *One of my clients identified major spending customers and held annual reviews with them. At these reviews they talked the customers through their spending pattern over the period, and shared a report about the customers purchasing over the last year. This included recommendations for saving money and information about industry developments. The customers loved these reviews and began to view the company as a trusted advisor, instead of just another supplier.*

The ultimate good customer is the one who is willing to recommend the company to other potential customers.

Not all customers are equal

PRINCIPLE: A company must focus on extending the time that its hard won customers continue to buy from them.

Some companies have challenges with growing customer lifetime. The revenue potential of a customer varies from industry to industry. For example, the revenue earned from a mobile phone customer over twelve months may look like this;

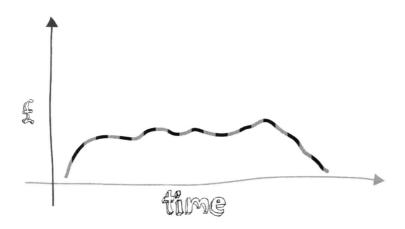

Compare this with someone buying a new car

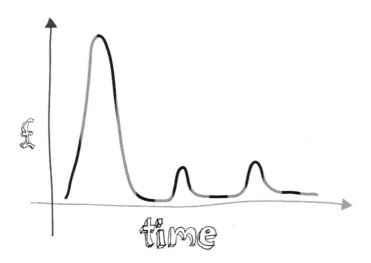

The challenge is to find ways to keep customers spending, and in a conversation with the company. Luckily, there are very few products that work in splendid isolation of any others.

A company should constantly search for related products and services that can be offered to customers.

> *I have worked with several swimming pool builders' pool building clients. A swimming pool is the sort of high value purchase you only make once or twice in a lifetime.*
>
> *One way pool builders overcome this 'lumpy revenue' profile is to offer service packages that keep the pool clean and ready for customers to swim in. The customer has an option to pay this charge annually, quarterly or monthly, and it gives the pool company a chance to smooth its revenue, and equally importantly, maintain a relationship with their customer.*

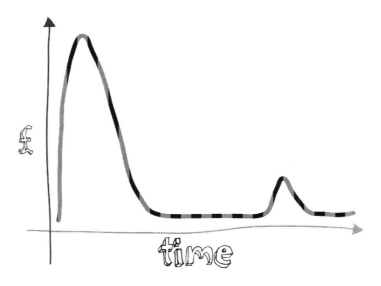

What else?

Imagine you are put in charge of a shop and told to increase sales. On the first day you take a look round and you find a bunch of really cool products in the stockroom that are not on display. What would you do?

Customers associate companies with the products they buy from them. They may be unaware of the full range of what the company sells. Looking at what each customer is and is not buying can provide opportunities to grow customer lifetime value. Search for customers who are similar, and then look at what they buy from the company.

I get my clients to prepare a customer/product matrix, as below. This allows them to search for patterns and identify further revenue potential from their existing customers.

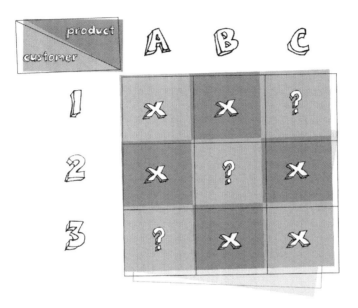

Where did they go?

PRINCIPLE: A company must identify good customers that are going to leave and make efforts to keep them.

Growing the customer base is important, but so is making sure that you are not losing customers.

It is expensive and hard work to acquire new customers. What if, in spite of sterling work by the sales force, the customer base never seems to get any bigger? Perhaps the company is pouring water into a leaky bucket. Some customers don't like dealing with the company and they leave.

Some companies struggle to know when a customer has gone. Not every product or service has an 'off' button; a trigger that notifies you that a customer has left.

> *In the mobile phone company it was relatively easy to know that a customer under contract had left. The contract expired and they didn't renew it. Pay as you Go mobile phones users, on the other hand, don't have contracts. They are free to switch to another operator at will. As there was no monitoring in place it was impossible to detect who had left. A minimum usage definition was developed and a reporting system put in place so that we were able to figure out how many active customers we actually had.*

Identifying when a customer has stopped buying from the company, or is showing signs that they are about to stop, is an important function that often gets overlooked.

This **CUSTOMER CHURN** is often expressed as a percentage e.g. 23% of contracts did not renew.

The intelligence that can be gleaned by understanding why customers leave is gold dust. It can be used to refine products, pricing, or delivery processes.

If you don't ask, you won't know where improvement is needed.

Why do customers stop buying?

Research into why customers switch suppliers claim that 68% (BSS) change for nothing more than 'perceived indifference'. In other words, they didn't think that the company was bothered whether they stayed or left.

PRINCIPLE: If you lose a customer, it's because you didn't do the right things to keep them.

This is excellent news. It means that by taking an active interest in customers and staying in touch it is possible to significantly reduce churn.

One of my clients sells a service to other businesses that is based on a three-year contract. The sales force was increasingly struggling to sign new customers and there was a lot of focus on improving their performance. Early on in the coaching programme we were discussing the customer base, and I asked what the renewal rate of customers reaching the end of contract was. The number was significantly lower than had been assumed, and the insight drove the directors to gradually transform their business and put more focus on customer service, particularly ensuring customers were using the service. 'Lack of use' was seen as a critical indicator of a potential non-renewal. Proactive contacts with customers were introduced when usage dropped.

Win back their love, unless they are ugly

It is always worth trying to re-engage customers who stop buying. At the very least a company can find out why and may be able to tempt them back. Remember, they loved the company once.

It is intriguing to understand customers who bought once and then stopped. This can point to:

- good sales pitches let down by sub-standard product and service
- good product and service let down by an over-promise in the sales pitch

Either way the customer's expectation was not met so they didn't buy again, and unless asked, they may never reveal the answers.

In the mobile phone company there was a department dedicated to retentions. When a customer called in to cancel their contract they were put through to the retentions team. This team was carefully chosen and trained to try and persuade the customer to stay with us. They had a matrix of offers that they used to try and keep the customer, based on the customer's lifetime value and the history of the relationship they had with us.

Keeping in contact

PRINCIPLE: Keep in touch with customers, because the competition will be trying to.

The idea that nearly 70% (BSS) of customer churn is as a result of perceived indifference raises an important question. How often should a company connect with its customers?

Ignoring normal order processing and queries, how often, and by what means, does the company communicate with its customers? A two-way flow of information between customer and company is invaluable. It can provide insight about what is happening in the lives of customers, what is exciting them and what is worrying them? This is all valuable feedback.

There is a trade-off to be made when deciding how, and how often, to contact customers. High value customers may have a dedicated account manager; others may simply be on a monthly email newsletter database. When in doubt, ask customers and then put in place a contact programme that meets their needs.

Ugly customers

There are some customers that a company would happily see appearing in the churn figures. The ones who drain customer services and account managers time and energy, pay when it suits them and put ridiculous demands on the delivery capabilities of the company. They are unprofitable, a huge drain and a waste of energy, so send them a goodbye card when they do go. Even better, identify them and pass them on to the competition yourself.

MECHANIC FIVE - DO ALL THE ABOVE IN A WAY THAT MAKES A MARGIN

PRINCIPLE: The ultimate financial goal of a company is to make a profit margin that reflects the level of investment made in the company.

The goal of a company is to create a surplus of money. A profit margin is made when there is a positive gap between the value of sales and the costs the business incurred. Margin can be expressed as a number, e.g., we made £50,000 profit, or as a % of sales, e.g., we made 25% profit.

PRINCIPLE: increasing sales and/or reducing costs can improve Margin.

There are four levers to improve profit margin.

INCREASE SALES

1. Charge more for products
2. Sell more products

REDUCE COSTS

3. Lower production or buying cost of product
4. Lower fixed cost

Charge more

One of the first questions that I ask a new small business client is 'when did you last raise your prices?' This is a nifty little trick I learnt in coaching school to quickly pay back my clients investment in coaching. Most small business owners get anxious about increasing prices for fear of losing customers, so they don't bother. Enter business coach from stage left, raise prices and instantly achieves god-like status amongst their clients. It is an over-simplification that you can often get away with.

PRINCIPLE - The ultimate arbiter of how much your products should cost is the customer and the market.

A customer will pay what they think the product, and a relationship with the company, is worth to them. This perception is based on:

- quality of the product

- reputation of the company

- service they get

- convenience

- comparison to competition

- the brand

Based on an emotionally loaded assessment of your company the customer will establish a perceived value. If the price meets or beats this, they will buy. If it doesn't, they will either walk away or try to negotiate.

> *"If you lose on price it's because you suck at sales" – Jeffery Gitomer*

Decisions to buy are led by gut feelings. Research suggests that 80% of a buying decision is emotionally led and 20% (BSS) logic. If anything, logic is often just used to justify gut feel.

The prices of products should be continually reviewed and tested to establish where the edge of perceived value is.

If some customers stop buying as a result of price increases, the impact is not as significant as it might seem. If a company sells a product at a gross margin of 40%, and raises the price of the product by 10%, they could lose 20% of their customers for the product, without any impact on their bottom line.

This table illustrates the percentage of business that could be lost without any bottom line impact, based on various price increase/margin scenarios.

margin

	20%	30%	40%	50%	60%
2%	9%	6%	5%	4%	3%
10%	33%	25%	20%	17%	14%
14%	41%	32%	26%	22%	19%
20%	50%	40%	33%	29%	25%
25%	56%	45%	38%	33%	29%

price increase

The magic pricing products

Some products are more price-sensitive to customers than others, particularly ones that are bought regularly, or that customers have to buy but don't want to buy. The cost of these products can influence a customer's 'feel' for your pricing in general. For my lighting wholesaler, there are some everyday products that are routinely purchased. Customers know how much they should pay for them and so raising these prices could result in an exodus of customers.

If customers use comparisons, it is helpful to know what, and how, they compare. This can educate a company's pricing.

> One of my employers was a utility company and comparison sites were widely used by their customers to save money. The pricing team worked out what usage levels these websites were using to demonstrate pricing differences (the cost of gas or electric

is dependent on your consumption rate). We changed our pricing so that when you hit the 'average' usage level they were using to measure, we were the most competitive. If you went slightly above that threshold, our price was higher so we made money with the upper echelon of customers, whilst remaining competitive on the websites.

Increasing sales volume

Selling more products can increase profit and margin. Companies often try to increase sales volumes by reducing the price. This can stimulate demand, but the full impact needs to be understood.

If the same company as before cut prices of its product by 10%, they will need to get an additional 33% of business just to cover the cost of the price reduction.

margin

price discount	20%	30%	40%	50%	60%
2%	11%	7%	5%	4%	3%
10%	100%	50%	33%	25%	20%
14%	233%	88%	54%	39%	30%
20%		200%	100%	67%	50%
25%		500%	167%	100%	71%

Demand is better stimulated using marketing, or by adding value to the existing product.

I recently had the necessity to buy a new vacuum cleaner. The model I bought was the same price in all the stores I looked at, but in one there was the offer of a tool set worth £65, reduced

*to £30. I am a sucker for a bargain so went with this deal.
The chances are the store made little or no margin on the
accessory set, but got the full margin for the vacuum cleaner
itself. In my perception as the customer, I saved £35 and now
cannot find any part of my property that cannot be reached and
blasted with the vacuum.*

Lower production or buying costs

The cheaper it is for a company to buy the things it needs to make
products, or to buy stock, the better the margin it has the potential to make.

Getting cheaper stock, raw materials, or components will often mean
buying, or committing to, larger volumes. This can involve tying up cash
and additional storage costs.

Attempts can be made to reduce prices through, negotiation, but anything
other than a win-win plan with suppliers will ultimately fail.

Good purchasing is about working with suppliers to engineer value in a way
that enables the company and its suppliers to make margins. This extends
beyond discussions of price, but takes a bigger view of the relationship, as a
company should with its customers.

For companies involved in production, or those who sell time for money,
there is also the continual drive for greater efficiency in the manufacture of
products or delivery of services as a means to grow margin. This may mean
investing in technologies, better design and scheduling of production, or
looking at alternative means of production and delivery, such as sub-
contracting and outsourcing. Inevitably, there are trade-offs that have to be
considered in any changes, particularly how it affects the shape of the
margin triangle.

Lower fixed costs

The fourth lever is to reduce the fixed costs in the business. Depending on
accounting policies, the biggest operating cost for most businesses is payroll
and the associated costs of people in the company. Inevitably, this is a cost
that many companies keep under tight control. It is also the one that is
targeted when the business is not performing.

Keeping costs under constant scrutiny is important for any company. I was annually set a 15% cost reduction challenge in my operational role. These challenges required creative thinking to deliver without damaging the company.

Understanding the impact of reductions is vital. If costs are removed from 'front line' customer facing or impacting teams, the results can be seen and measured quite clearly. Back office reductions seem to have little or no immediate effect, because the impact takes longer to become visible, or can be an opportunity cost that never becomes fully visible.

PRINCIPLE: Fixed cost reductions that are not resulting from leveraged solutions are never impact free.

Margin leakage

If pricing is set correctly, the cost of sales is understood and operating costs are fixed down, a company should automatically hit its target profit margin, shouldn't it?

I'm afraid not. Profit margin is affected by many variables.

> One day I was discussing margins with one of my clients who has a Quantity Surveying practice. His business is a classic 'time for money' trade. He submits a proposal based on how many days of effort the job will take, adds his margin, and bingo. We were looking at jobs recently completed and all of them were coming in on budget. If he quoted ten days they were taking ten days. The job should have been delivered with margin bang on target. Yet when we looked at the profit and loss account, the margin was a fraction of what was budgeted. There was a leak.

> When we looked at the numbers, one of the challenges was that the team was only utilized for 70% of their working week. The other 30% was made up of some rework and non-productive time. Virtually the entire margin in the jobs was being lost.

> The owner set a target utilization rate for the team that enabled the business to make the required margin, and introduced

utilization rate to his business dashboard.

Utilization - the missing margin link

Getting the most out of people and resources is important for any company, particularly those where people costs make up a significant percentage of their cost of sales.

Keeping the profit margin on target requires that lots of complicated variables work properly. Margin leakage can happen in very strange ways. Here are my own personal greatest hits that I uncovered as an auditor and a business coach over the years.

Discounting and pricing errors - Discretionary, unplanned price reductions and pricing errors.

Errors and rework - Time and materials to correct faulty products, or sending the wrong product to the customer.

Waste materials - Raw materials wasted in production.

Billing errors - Failing to bill a customer for all of the products they have received.

Theft/Fraud - Fraud by employees and customers will occur when the right checks and balances are not in place.

Damages and write-offs - Damage to stored products and the write-off of 'out of date' or obsolete stock.

Returns - Failing to account for products and materials returned from customer, and to suppliers.

Collection of discounts – Failing to collect discounts due from suppliers.

Quotation and pricing errors - Getting the price or estimates in proposals wrong.

Over servicing - Giving the customer more than they paid for.

'Bling' costs - Gold plated staplers are not necessary in most businesses.

Industry processes - If a company operates in a regulated industry, or has shared industry processes, margin can be impacted by rules and processing errors outside of the company's control.

Currency fluctuations - When billing and/or payment for materials is in a different currency, exchange rate movements can either enhance or erode margin.

The wobbly margin

> *The utility company I worked for had a unique and complex margin problem. The problem was, we couldn't make the units of gas that we billed our customers for and the units of gas that the industry deemed we had used, balance.*
>
> *We figured out how much gas our customers were using by either getting a meter read or having the billing system provide an estimated bill for the customer. Every property had a unique meter reference number.*
>
> *We were given a figure of how much gas our customers were deemed to have used by the company that transported the gas and managed the pipes. They held records of which meter reference numbers were allocated to which gas supplier. Each meter reference number had an annual quantity (AQ) assigned to it. This was based on the previous year's consumption and once set, was fixed for twelve months. If the overall figure of gas used in the system was bigger than all the combined AQ's, then the difference would be divided across the suppliers based on their market share %.*
>
> *As you are reading you are probably beginning to see how there was a mild chance of margin leakage, except this wasn't mild. In one year this imbalance wiped £20m from the company's margin. This huge value was made up of a combination of:*

- *Discrepancies resulting from billing driven by our estimations*
- *Differences between actual customer consumption and the AQ set the previous year (consumption was slowly falling so previous quantities would tend, on average, to be over-inflated)*

- *Customers switching suppliers and their records getting 'stuck' in the cross industry process*

- *Cock-ups resulting from a recent migration to a new billing system that had left thousands of customers unbilled because they were stuck in our systems between actual customer consumption*

- *Gas leaks and theft of gas from the system*

- *Accounting adjustments made to try and smooth out the impact of the imbalance on the monthly profit and loss (the number had a habit of fluctuating wildly from month to month)*

- *Vacant properties where the meter had not been disconnected.*

So you can see how significant a problem margin leakage can become for a company if not controlled and understood.

A profitable company should, after making sales and taking costs out, be left with a surplus of cash in the bank, right?

If only life were that simple. There is a difference between profit and cash.

MECHANIC SIX - MANAGE ALL OF THE CASH IN AND OUT OF THE BUSINESS

PRINCIPLE: A company needs to have cash available to fund its continuing operations

> *"Turnover is vanity, profit is sanity, cash is reality"* - *every businessman that ever lived*

Cash is the oxygen of business. Pretty much any company that goes out of business does so at the point it runs out of cash to continue its operations. It is for this reason that finance teams will have a rolling forecast of the flow of cash in and out of the company.

If you started a company and made sales of £100 with costs of £60 in June, when I go to check your bank account I would expect to find £40, right? WRONG

This transaction would appear on the profit and loss report as follows:

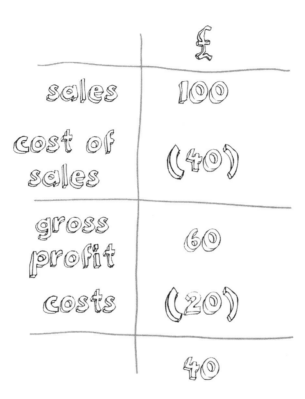

	£
sales	100
cost of sales	(40)
gross profit	60
costs	(20)
	40

In fact, whilst the sale and the cost of sale appear in the June profit and loss report, the actual movement of cash relating to these transactions can be quite different.

Cash timing

Many of the companies I worked for and coached had product delivery cycles that could take over a month, and they purchased stock or manufactured in volumes that were economic, as opposed to just when the customer wanted it. The movement of cash operated to a different timescale to the creation of profit.

Using the example above let's look at the actual cash movements.

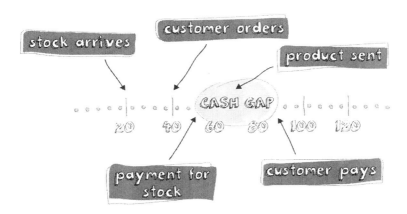

1. Stock or raw material are purchased
2. The customer orders
3. Payment is made for stock or raw materials
4. Product is sent to the customer
5. The customer pays

You can see here that there is a period of time between the materials being purchased and when the customer pays for the product. This is the CASH GAP.

The shape and duration of the cash gap varies across industries and companies.

In an ideal world a company would want a cash gap like this:

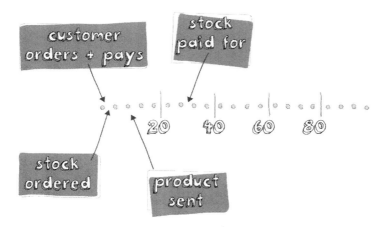

1. Customer orders and pays
2. Stock or raw materials are purchased
3. Product is sent to the customer
4. Payment is made for stock or raw materials

This would be a fully funded cash gap. The money to fund the product is received 'up-front'. The company would always have money in the bank provided they were making sales. Large retailers of fast moving lines such as food, with volume buying power and slick inventory management, often create a positive cash gap.

Understanding the cash gap is important for a company because it has to have sufficient cash to fund the gap, either through having reserves or borrowing. Both of these options carry an opportunity cost. Reserves could be used to fund further growth and borrowing incurs interest, which eats into profit margins.

> *One of my swimming pool building clients did a lot of*
> *installations as part of larger construction projects. The pool*
> *build timetable was subject to delays and rescheduling based on*
> *progress with the wider project. Payments were made by the*
> *main contractor to a pre-determined submission timetable. The*

challenge was that the business had high fixed costs to meet, so even with a volume of on-going projects, there were often periods where there was little revenue coming in. The owner often had to fund the business through these periods with personal money and would get very upset and frustrated, claiming that the team was not managing the projects and the payment submissions properly. He refused to entertain the idea of other short term funding, such as an overdraft facility.

To me it looked more like a cost of operating in the sector that they did. It was unlikely industry payment processes would change, and there was a limit to the improvements that could be made internally. A better approach was for them to understand and manage the company within this constraint.

Some companies will always have to live with a degree of 'feast and famine' in their cash flow. It is the cost of operating in some industries and markets.

Minding the gap

PRINCIPLE: Good cash flow control is a function of speeding up cash inflows and slowing down outflows.

A company will do what it can, subject to what the customer wants and suppliers are prepared to work with, to optimize its cash gap through a combination of:

- **Speeding up the money coming in** by having fast invoicing and strong credit management

- **Slowing down the money going out** by negotiating extended credit terms with suppliers or tighter management of stock levels

There are trade-offs with managing the cash gap. It is possible to alienate customers by being too heavy handed with credit management. Similarly, suppliers can become unwilling to supply if payment delays are excessive as it creates a cash gap problem for them.

I started to coach a printing company. During our first session the owners informed me of just how dire the financial situation was. They were financially hedge hopping (flying far too close to the ground) and had used up their overdraft. If some more work didn't come in within a few weeks, they were going to hit the ground. I asked about how much money the business was owed and they didn't know. I gave 24 hours to produce a schedule of completed work that had not been invoiced for, and invoices sent to customers that had not been paid.

The following day I visited them again and the schedule showed £10k worth of work waiting to be invoiced for, and over £50k outstanding with customers, some of it overdue by months. I made them stand up and walk out to the front of the building where I looked up at the building and said, "Well, where is the sign?"

They looked at me bemused, so I pointed to the signage. "I can't see the word bank in the description of your company. Go and get that money." The business was back on financial track two weeks later.

What to do with the surplus

The surplus cash created by company activities can be used in a number of ways:

- Expansion of the business through new products and into new markets

- Acquisition of other companies that complement its activities

- Payback debt that the company owes

- Returned to shareholders in the form of share dividends

- Invested in improving the organization, creating a more leveraged business

It is this organizational improvement to which we will turn our attention next.

MECHANIC SEVEN - ORGANISATION

PRINCIPLE: A company is a collection of systems and people, organized into a structure that enables it to serve customers and make profit

Once a successful way of making money has been found, the obvious thing to do would be to continue adding people and facilities to keep it growing, wouldn't it?

There are advantages and disadvantages to scale. Size enables the economies of buying and manufacturing in large volume. It enables the creation of specialist teams and jobs, which drives further efficiency.

As the organisation structure grows, the cost of managing and coordinating what is happening increases. It also becomes much harder to quickly react to changes in what customers and the market want, so opportunities get missed.

It makes sense instead, to focus on improving the efficiency and effectiveness of the company using the principle of leverage. Leveraging enables a company to continually achieve more without increasing costs and complexity.

PRINCIPLE: A company creates leverage by continually improving so it achieves better results with fewer resources.

Leverage is applied in three areas, the company's processes, structure and people.

Processes

PRINCIPLE: Processes are the way things get done. The extent to which these processes are understood, documented, and followed will determine the extent to which the company performs consistently or inconsistently

A process can be recorded as a checklist, procedure note, flowchart, step by step picture guide, manual, pop up box on a computer screen, video or sound recording. The way they are documented is NOT important. Documenting them is.

Company's processes are part of its intellectual property. They translate how it wants to serve its customers and generate profit into consistent actionable steps.

The more complicated activities become, the more necessity there is for checklists and procedures. People have a limited ability to remember so things will get forgotten, or done incorrectly, in anything but the simplest of tasks.

Processes will tend to change over time if not managed. People will seek out shortcuts under pressure. New people will find their own way of doing things.

> *One of the most well-known and easily observed systemized organizations is McDonalds. The whole business runs to detailed systems and instructions, even down to how a specific burger is assembled. The extent of systemization has allowed them to recruit young untrained employees at low cost, and quickly get them trained up to a level of competence. It is this systemization, coupled with a highly organized supply chain that enables them to achieve high volume throughput, consistency of product, low costs and maintain a good margin.*

A process is a baseline of performance. From this point improvements can be made. Processes continually evolve so that they become better for the customer and more efficient for the business.

Technology and automation create critical leverage points for many businesses, by reducing the number of people needed to operate the company, and maintaining consistency. Computer systems and automated machinery, when correctly configured, will deliver consistent results without the risk of human error or oversight.

> *The most amazing example of leverage I was involved in was early in my career with the food retailer. When I first joined the company, stock was distributed to stores either directly from suppliers (if it had a short shelf life), or via ambient or frozen product warehouses that were positioned strategically around the country. One of the first projects I was involved in was the rollout of their composite distribution system.*

The small distribution centres were replaced by huge, new distribution centres that had three separate chambers for ambient, chilled, and frozen products. All deliveries were re-routed into the composite distribution centres. Store orders were picked in the warehouse and then loaded onto Lorries that had sealable compartments to hold ambient, frozen, and chilled products at the required temperature. There were, of course, some teething problems, but they were relatively minor.

The savings in store headcount, delivery costs, in-store space, and wastage were huge. Two of the new distribution centres were run in-house and the remainder outsourced to agency distribution companies to enable further productivity improvements to be measured.

The composite system also provided the platform to support the future growth of the company, which at that time, was rolling out over twenty new superstores each year.

Technology and automation has created, and will continue to create, opportunity for leverage in companies. This enables them to improve the customer experience, speed up the processing of sales, reduce running costs, and generate information to provide business insight.

The exception to the rule

No system is infallible. There will always be exceptions resulting from errors and non-standard sales. The 80/20 rule applies. At least 80% of the transactions a company processes should pass seamlessly through the business, virtually untouched. The other 20% may become stuck and require a person to take an action to get the 'pig moving through the python' again. Remaining in control of the volume of exceptions, and keeping transactions running freely through systems, is important.

I joined the Utility Company shortly after the implementation of a new customer management and billing system. I was asked to join because of my experience of managing complex billing systems. The implementation had been a bit of a balls-up, (understatement), and was causing some serious operational difficulties. The customer billing system worked by processing meter readings from properties, applying them to the customer account, and then producing or estimating a customer bill.

As soon as customers were migrated across into the new system a very high volume of exceptions was created, mainly related to a check the system did of the plausibility of the meter read (based on historic readings). These volumes had not been anticipated and so there weren't enough resources to clear the exceptions.

Lots of customer accounts became stuck, and then to make matters worse, the exceptions started to impact each other. Before long the entire system was out of control and it took years to recover.

Structure

PRINCIPLES: A company creates a structure for people to work within, aligned to the tasks that need to be done. This structure continually develops to meet the changing needs of the company.

Start-ups and small businesses can operate effectively with an 'all hands to the pump' structure. A brand new start up may only have the owner who has to fulfil all of the roles of the business.

There comes a point, typically when a business has around six employees, where specialization begins to emerge. People fall into specific roles, initially based on three areas, sales, production, and administration. This enables people to be individually accountable for the outcomes in specific areas of the business. This is the birth of an organization structure.

As the company grows, so does the structure. The structures grow both horizontally and vertically.

Horizontal growth

The core business disciplines of sales, marketing, delivery, customer service, and accounting grow as the company grows. The size of these teams is a function of the market, customer base, and the leverage applied through automation and systems.

Support functions emerge to provide the company with specific support, advice, and information, such as IT, human resources, finance analysis, facilities management, investor relations, legal, and regulatory. These disciplines are transferable and can often be outsourced, because whilst important, they are not 'core' and the technical content of the activities is largely generic (applicable to any company).

Oversight functions also emerge, such as quality, internal audit, and risk management. These functions support the board by ensuring the business is running smoothly and to help them be confident that the company is running properly.

Vertical growth

As teams within the structure grow, there becomes a need for more leaders to manage and supervise people. This results in vertical growth of the organization. This growth is required because there is a limit to how many direct reports one person is able to manage. This is the 'span of control'. The numbers often suggested as the maximum span of control is between 7 and 13 (BSS) individuals. This is dependent on the style of management required and the type of work. If all of a manager's direct reports do a similar role with the same responsibilities and reporting, then the span of control can, in theory, increase.

> *One of the companies I worked for underwent a significant restructure in the early '90s, as did many large organizations. This was at the time when Business Process Re-engineering and 'empowerment' were highly fashionable. In theory, these admirable organisation design tools meant that through better systems, and even more critically, information flows, it was possible to create efficiency by reducing the numbers of management layers and support functions required.*

> *Process teams were set up and after six months reported back. The results were a shock to the Board. The net findings were that to be more efficient required MORE investment, instead of less. With this information to hand the board did exactly what you would expect them to do. They cut out the management layers and reduced the support functions anyway.*

Now the company went on to great success, but something changed at that point. This period marked the start of the era of overwhelm in the management team, which has led this, and many other companies, to the point they are today. All of the productive hours of focus and scrutiny delivered in those redundant roles had been doing something.

PRINCIPLE: Fixed cost reductions that are not resulting from leverage are never impact free.

Structure types

The companies I have worked for have adopted an array of different high-level organization structures. I have worked with product division structures where each product category is run like a separate business, country divisions where each country is run like a separate business, matrix organizations that try to adopt a structure that enables responsibility for product and region to be managed, and centralized businesses with a single company structure.

I have learnt two things about organization design:

1. The structure is NEVER the issue. The degree of centralization/decentralization, and how that impacts each individual's sense of power and status, is ALWAYS the issue.

2. The structure is NEVER the issue. Tinkering and endless re-organizing solves nothing. It simply moves problems around.

   I worked for a major drinks manufacturer that was structured into branded companies, each of which was run autonomously. One of the cool things the CEO did was to hold a lunch once a week, where a number of junior executives were invited along. I was lucky enough to get invited to one of these. The only golden rule was that you had to have a question to ask him.

   I had been involved with a project that was looking at the centralization of the purchasing of certain key commodities across the group of companies. One of these was glass (as you can imagine a company made up of major drink brands gets through a LOT of glass). My question was as follows:

"The analysis across the group shows that there are tens of millions of pounds to be saved by the company each year if we were to consolidate our glass purchasing across the whole group, instead of each company buying its own, what stops a decision like this being made?"

The CEO told me that every year the Head of Purchasing presented the Board of Directors with an analysis of the potential savings that could be generated by centralizing procurement. Every year the board debated it, and at face value, it seemed like a no brainer decision. But the Board was also aware of the trade-off that they would have to make. He went on, "When we review the results of any one of the companies in the group we can look the CEO in the eye knowing that they are solely responsible for their results. Every line on the profit and loss account is under their control. There is nowhere to hide. As soon as we remove control of any aspect of the profit and loss account, we dilute their accountability. So in spite of the formidable financial benefits, the board has, so far, never voted to adopt a centralised purchasing structure."

PRINCIPLE: There is no such thing as a perfect structure. When a company restructures, all it does is move the tension points around.

The rise of the silos

With scale, people and teams become increasingly remote from each other. Each function is under pressure to deliver its responsibilities. This can result in dysfunctional behaviour.

Customers and processes do not respect organizational boundaries, in fact quite the opposite. They cut across departments and silo's and for most processes to work requires the efforts of many people sat in different departments doing their bit. It is at these intersections that things are most likely to go wrong.

As an auditor, it is remarkable how many times I have identified a system failure and been met with the words, 'the problem is the other department are not doing this properly', or 'the other department are not meeting their service level agreement'. If you want to find the point where processes are most vulnerable, then you need to look at the interfaces between different departments and systems.

The commonest challenges arise between:

- Sales and Operations

- Customer Services and Operations

- IT and everyone

- Finance and everyone

As the problems compound people become defensive, and rather than deal with the problem at the point it occurs, 'up and around' loops begin to form. A problem gets escalated up a departmental structure, across to another department, and down the line, and on, and on, and on.

To overcome these problems, some companies bring in roles to co-ordinate activities (processes, programs, and projects) that cut across silo boundaries. These roles attempt to get everyone playing nicely. This can often introduce more people, more meetings, more reports, and more problems.

Companies begin to slow down and become almost paralyzed with their inability to solve problems or introduce anything new.

Here comes the treacle

> *I attended a conference for top 100 managers with one of my employers. The CEO, frustrated by the slowness of the progress of key initiatives for the organizations success, berated us all. His words stuck with me. "Every time we embark on an initiative to improve things for our customers, it is like wading through treacle and things move at a snail's pace, if at all".*

The treacle slows things down. Everyone needs to be involved in every decision and personal agendas, overwhelm and silo mentalities drive a lack of big picture thinking. This creates rocks and obstacles that block progress.

How many great ideas have been slowly strangled by everyone being too busy, slow decision-making and bureaucracy? Rapid execution of the RIGHT things requires new thinking

The problem is not structural or process; it is ALWAYS the behaviour of people. The behaviour of people is the KEY leverage point

PRINCIPLE: The best processes and structure in the world will never make ungrounded people great.

People

I had been thinking about how I could best support my clients with managing teams simply. There is so much horse shit written about leadership and team dynamics that I was having trouble coming up with something simple and elegant. Then one of my clients lost his cool one day with one of his team. He grabbed a flip chart and a marker and drove home. At home he inadvertently created an awesome tool for managing teams, which I nicked. I call it the team audit.

He wrote out what he saw as the strengths and weaknesses of each of his team members, and then scored each employee based on a scale of 1-10. He then spent his time thinking about a plan to:

- *Give his high performers more responsibility*

- *Shift his 'average' performers*

- *Deal with his low performers*

At our next coaching session he took me through the results and his plan. I added a few finesses and it became the team audit, which I now do with all my new clients.

Most teams in companies look like this:

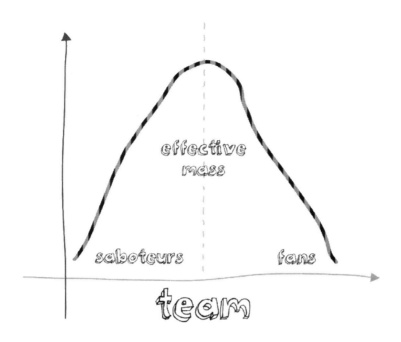

There are always high performers who enjoy their jobs and would happily recommend working for their company. There is the performing mass who do a good job and are productive, and there are saboteurs; the poison apples. They spend their days quietly undermining the business, complaining about everything, and generally investing energy in trying to bring everyone down to their level.

I can spot a saboteur a mile away, because I have been one myself. I have been in roles where I bought into the wrong story and started to hang around and conspire with all the other negative people. I can recognize the signs.

The only other finesse I added to the team audit was to score two aspects of an individual: performance and attitude. Performance is how good they are at performing the actual job, and attitude is the manner in which they behave while performing it.

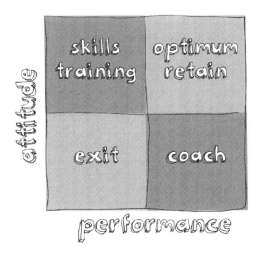

The idea is to keep the curve moving towards the right and there are a number of ways to achieve this:

- Move the mid performers to fans
- Move the saboteurs to mid performers;
- Sack the saboteurs

On/off the bus

PRINCIPLE: A company should only have employees who want to work there and are willing to always do their best

> *"When you've finally exhausted all carrots and sticks, relax and remember some folks are just dicks"*

If you had a car that kept breaking down you would take it to a garage and get it fixed. If after a few visits to the garage it still wasn't working, you would probably change the car. Perhaps it wasn't the right car for the job you wanted it to do, or maybe the job you want the car to do has changed and it is no longer fit for purpose.

A good question for a company to ask of its employees, and for its employees to ask themselves, is:

Are you on the bus or off the bus?

If people are on the bus, then they believe in the company and want to do a good job. If they are not on the bus, then they should be looking for a company and a career that would fire them up.

It is possible to have people on the right bus, but in the wrong seat.

> *The first big audit team that I worked in had a small team of secretaries. One of them was a classic poor employee. She had lots of sickness, would routinely arrive late looking like she had been dragged through a hedge, and had a real attitude. It was almost impossible to get anything done if she didn't like you. The question, "how are you today" was guaranteed to illicit a pained and depressing response.*
>
> *Then one day she got another job. The whole team was delighted and the best thing was that the Human Resources department had taken her on, in a supervisory role. The irony that HR's own interviews had not unearthed what a loser she was remained a source of mirth in the department for some time.*
>
> *I met her a few months later. It was 7:30 in the morning and I bumped into her in the corridor of head office. I was shocked to see her at work so early and I asked her how she was getting on. She told me she loved the job, but was finding the twelve-hour day hard work! She had recruited and set up a new team of administrators, trained them and got the whole department working really well.*

A company owes it to their employees, and an employee owes it to their company, to find out what they are really good at and to point them towards this. People who are supreme performers do work that they enjoy. It is that simple.

Getting the right people

PRINCIPLE: When recruiting, there are only two possible decisions; Hell yeah or No.

It all starts with recruiting the right people. Some companies are lazy recruiters taking on anyone with a pulse. People are the ultimate leverage point in any business and there is no more important decision than whether to take on an individual or not.

> *I was discussing the recent departure of one of my client's management team with them (it is not unusual for at least one resignation in a business when I start working with them). My client was reflecting on what had gone wrong, so I asked him what he thought after he had originally interviewed him. "I remember thinking, he'll do..." As soon as he said the words, he learnt the lesson.*

'Someone will do' is **not**, and **will never be**, appropriate criteria for recruiting anybody to do anything.

It is possible to test for 'Hell Yeah' by:

- having a detailed application form

- spending more time in interview and searching for evidence that they 'have done' or 'could do' what the company wants them to

- getting more than one person to interview them, including people they will have working for them and colleagues they will need to interact with

- running psychometric tests and aptitude tests for the roles they are applying for

Performance Management

Leveraging people requires that their performance is measured and then improvement made so that they continually get better at what they do.

What is good performance?

Someone who is performing well at their job does two things;

- They do what they were supposed to do, in the way they were supposed to do it, with the resources they were given to do it (PERFORMANCE)

- They did what they were supposed to do in a manner that left their customers, suppliers, colleagues and team happy (ATTITUDE)

The measurement of performance should be against clearly defined standards of performance (cost, time, quality, etc.), or measurable goals or actions

The measurement of attitude should be based on expected standards of behaviours and measured by feedback from the people they are required to connect with.

Dealing with poor performance

There are only four reasons why people don't perform in their role:

1. **They don't know what they are supposed to do, or why** - If someone has not been given enough instructions, or shown how to do something, they will probably give it their best attempt with the limited knowledge they have. If they don't know why they need to do something, this makes even guessing how to do it challenging. When this doesn't match up to the company's expectation, this shows as poor performance.

2. **They don't want to do it, or do it in the way that is expected of them** - If someone truly doesn't want to do something, then they either need to change their attitude to their role or go and work somewhere else.

3. **They don't have the skills, time, or resource to do it** - If this is the reason why someone isn't performing then you have a choice. Either free the constraint or bring someone else that is able to do the job with what is available.

4. **There are no consequences to them doing the job as you want it done** - If there isn't a sufficient carrot available to incentivise people, or the implications of doing the job incorrectly are not understood, or felt, don't be surprised when people don't perform.

"Men will die for ribbons" - Napoleon Bonaparte

It is rare to find someone that deliberately sets out to do a bad job. Some do exist, but they normally stick out like a sore thumb in a team and don't last long before they are discovered.

Managing performance is not an annual appraisal; it is a daily and hourly habit.

Noticing and acknowledging when people have done a great job goes a long way to getting more from people, simply because humans like to feel connected and appreciated. Similarly, correcting performance more often means coaching and supporting than it involves the issuance of a bollocking. Kindness ultimately secures better performance, because it reinforces an individual's grounding and connection.

PRINCIPLE: You will always get the people you deserve and the behaviours you tolerate

When I was training to be a business coach we were made to play volleyball every morning. As well as waking us up, it also provided a great opportunity to explore the dynamics of team working. I wrote some notes down after each game and at the end of the training course I made this list:

- *Team power outweighs individual power every time*

- *Accept that things change and stay in the game*

- *Coaching each other improves performance and understanding*

- *Passion counts and makes a difference*

- *Sometimes you need to be tough on people*

- *Encouragement over chastisement*

- *Be honest, give feedback*

- *Never give up no matter what; winning a serve turns the game*

- *Allow people to take risks with their shots*

- *Own your shots*

Sometimes you have to lead from the front

A final word on leverage

"When we demand that our workers engage in a race to the bottom with any country willing to work faster and more robotically, we take something away from the people we work with" - *Seth Godin*

The drive to create leverage ultimately results in a high-risk trade off. Systemization, automation and the relentless drive for efficiency eventually begin to conflict with our desire to connect with others, and to express ourselves through our activities.

Customers want a good service and a personal touch to their interactions with a company. The standard of service and the convenience promised by large companies has, in many cases, been compromised by the drive for cheaper, to the point where all 'art' in the role is lost. The art is the employee's ability to express something of themselves through their work and their connections with colleagues and customers.

We deny employees their grounding, and then wonder why they become disengaged from their work and their company.

The ultimate leverage point for an organization is its people. As we shall see, grounded and connected people are not driven by the need to protect themselves from criticism or loss and they do not fear change. They operate from a place of intuition that no system can ever replicate and are driven by a deeper desire to make the right things happen for customers and colleagues. The company becomes an expression of the very humanity it serves and that exists within it. From this place, making a margin is the easy bit.

IDEA TWO - EXECUTION

The mechanics dictate the actions that companies have to take in order to be successful. At the junior levels of companies, people's actions are pre-prescribed by processes and timetables. Many roles have their day mapped out and there is little opportunity for choice. As someone advances through a company, or starts up a company, their use of the working day becomes increasingly discretionary.

The 'doing of tasks' and the 'following of processes' becomes new activities; observing, planning, controlling others, interpreting information, making decisions and implementing change. This requires new ideas and skills along with the self-discipline and control to make the best use of time. The habits of execution provide an operating framework for making choices, getting things done and monitoring progress.

There have been times over the course of my career where I have been devastatingly effective at taking action and times when I just could not be arsed. I have read books and been trained in countless time, project and productivity management courses. There were lots of good ideas, but none of them stayed with me beyond a week after I learnt them.

Instead I found myself defaulting back to my old habits. One of my habitual behaviours is to leave things to the last minute to do. I used to waste hours agonising over why I wasn't working on a board presentation until the night before.

My task planning consisted of notes made in a journal instead of a structured system. It was simply not good enough.

So what did I do to change? Absolutely nothing. In spite of my best efforts to make a lousy job of managing my activity, everything always got done, and I generally achieved all the objectives set for me.

This is because, whilst to the outsider (and for a good part of my life, myself) my strategies were poor, they WORKED FOR ME. To be good at execution requires that you:

- understand the principles that underpin execution

- find techniques to apply those principles that work for you

- create habits of behaviour so that you save energy (remembering to brush your teeth)

Until they are well formed, habits are vulnerable to crisis or panic. As soon as there is a problem, good habits are abandoned as we roll up our sleeves and heroically dive in, generally making problems even worse. This behaviour, whilst well meaning, is the beginning of a life on the hamster wheel.

> *Aircraft are flown using checklists. There are checklists for how to take off, how to fly, how to land, and how to refuel. The reason is that there are important things that have to be done consistently to be safe. Because there is a lot to remember a checklist is used to ensure that things don't get missed.*
>
> *There are checklists for emergencies as well. A simple emergency checklist I found online consists of five words: aviate, navigate, investigate, communicate, and secure.*
>
> *Why is aviate the first thing on an emergency checklist?*
>
> *Whatever's happening, the pilot must keep flying the plane. They must maintain height and keep the aircraft in the correct trim so that it continues to fly for as long as possible while they are dealing with the emergency. In the heat of panic, pilots have forgotten this with devastating consequences.*

Maintaining the habits of execution allows you to continue to show strong leadership and to keep the plane flying, no matter what is happening.

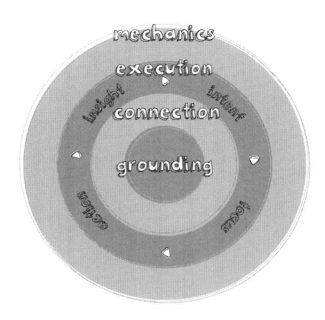

The four habits of execution are:

- Intent - the ability to 'see' the future outcome required and to build a bridge to cross the performance gap between 'there' and 'here'

- Focus - directing the resources you have with intensity onto achieving the future outcome. This means stopping things that are just not important ENOUGH

- Action - doing the things that need to be done

- Insight - continually measuring your progress towards the outcome and keeping your antennas out for changes that impact the company

As we look at each habit in turn, think about how you get things done. You will not find a list of strategies here. I am pointing you to principles so you can find improvements that fit with your working style.

HABIT ONE - INTENT

"It is not the strongest or the most intelligent who will survive but those who can best manage change." Charles Darwin

Intent - Determined to do something.

Change is a constant in any company. Whether a company is looking for growth or adapting to survive, it is in a state of perpetual evolution. There is always something to change, because no company can afford to stand still.

There is progression or regression - Status Quo no longer exists as an option (or a credible rock band).

The need to progress means that a gap always exists between current and desired performance.

Intent is the habit of creating and committing to a change plan, by creating a bridge between where you are, and where you need to be.

Given this context, it is obvious that people should embrace change, but once again our neurology throws barriers up.

"What kept me alive yesterday will keep me alive today". We all have this coding and it means that our default position when presented with change, even when we know it's positive, is to resist it at some level.

So to create change you need enough propulsion to break through the gravity of resistance that holds you where you are.

We are motivated to change by two main desires:

1. To stop bad stuff happening, i.e., if I don't do this I will get sacked
2. To make good things happen, i.e., if I do this my boss will pay me a bonus

It is easier to get people to act when they can CLEARLY see impending disaster.

Some people can also be motivated to 'go the extra mile' on the CLEAR promise of a better future.

The second type of motivation is in shorter supply than the first.

The most compelling driver of change is a blend of good stuff happening and bad stuff not happening.

To bridge the gap you need:

- A clear understanding of what 'there' might look like
- A clear understanding of what 'here' looks like
- An understanding of the gap between these two points
- A plan that bridges the gap

Step 1 - The Future's Bright

The first step towards change is to be clear about where you are heading. A more compelling vision can provide 'move toward' motivation that pulls the company forward.

One of my clients is a quantity surveyor. Whilst discussing how he delivered his service he showed me a drawing of a building that they were working on. The level of detail that went into the design was incredible. This enabled the building to be accurately costed. As we talked it occurred to me that barely any businesses have such a clear vision of what they are trying to create.

A desired future is often expressed as a goal, target, or outcome (an increase in sales/profit, launch of a new product, or an improvement to the experience your customers have).

Articulating the outcome is also important so that you know when you have arrived. With tangible targets this is easy, i.e., did we hit our sales targets? But what about improving the customer's experience? You could go on forever without realising you arrived months ago.

I worked for a fixed line operator who had embarked on a two-year project to implement a customer management system. When I became involved on the project team it was year four. The team were still sweeping up problems from the implementation that had happened eighteen months previously.

The chief technical officer and customer services director made a decision that sent a shock wave through the programme amidst huge protest from the project team, me included. They shut the project funding down. There were still things to be fixed and without the funding stream from the project new change requests would have to be raised and submitted for prioritization with everything else the business wanted to do. It was a disaster.

It was totally the right decision. The system was 80% operational and was working pretty well. There were more bugs and fixes required, but these were, in the main, not customer impacting and there were no more of them than in most of the company's systems. It was in a 'business as usual' state, but the project team was not prepared to accept it.

Research has shown a link between successful people and the presence of written goals. Goals that are SMART: Specific, Measurable, Achievable, Result-based, and Time lined.

Yet I know successful people who don't set goals and unsuccessful people who do set them. The importance of a goal is not in the setting of it, but in the actions taken in pursuit of achieving it.

Many of my clients find goals too abstract. They prefer to invest time in understanding the relationship between what they do and the results they get, and set action targets.

In my own business and life, I maintain a list of things I would like to achieve, but I don't feel the need to read them out loud to myself every day, or chant them while in the shower. I am aware of them, and I am aware of what I need to do in each day to move towards them.

Find what works for your company and for you.

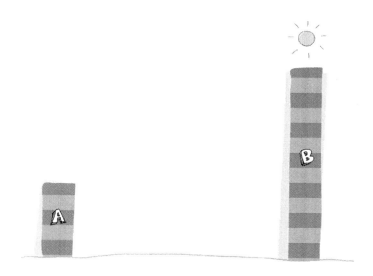

Step 2 - Confront Reality

The next step is to understand where the company is now. Confronting the reality of the current situation is critical. It enables the gap to be clearly understood as well as providing the 'move away' motivation to push you forward.

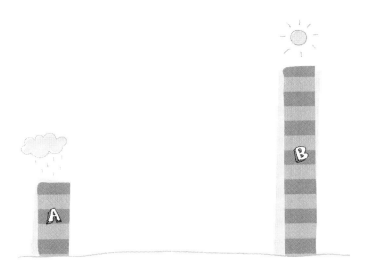

Understanding where you are will include looking at:

- What is working and what do you have at your disposal to use

- What is it not working and needs to improve

- What is happening in the marketplace that affects your ability to survive and grow

Step 3 - Mind the Gap (it's bigger than you think)

Where you are now is not where you will be in twelve months if you change nothing. If a company stands still, the market and the competition will continue to develop, leaving it behind.

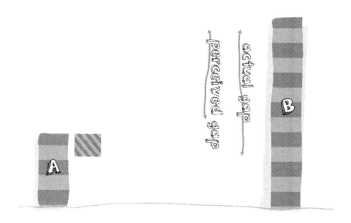

One of my clients is a lighting wholesaler. The introduction of LED technology is changing the industry. The historic robust revenue from their traditional product lines is eroding as companies transition to the new energy efficient technologies. It has not been an overnight change, but has now begun to gather pace. They are now a market leader in LED technology, which has kept their revenue growing, but they have had to fill a revenue gap created by the loss of sales in traditional lamps.

The gap between 'here' and 'there' is always bigger than it looks when you account for the 'do nothing' impact.

Step 4 - The Bridge

> *"In preparing for battle I have always found that plans are useless, but planning is indispensable."*
> Dwight Eisenhower

The bridge is a plan of building block actions that show the resources, skills, activities, knowledge, and connections required to make the planned transition.

Innovation may be required. Innovation is an area of performance that many people claim to struggle with, probably because they think they lack the ability to be innovative, or to solve problems (perhaps one of their teachers told them their art project lacked creativity and imagination). This is more horse shit.

We are naturally problem solvers. The size and structure of our brain reflects our innate ability to solve problems.

> *One of my clients had an away day with the team. At one point he was trying to elicit ideas from the team to improve the business margin. He was being met with a wall of silence. I took over and suggested that people imagine I was holding a gun to their head and would pull the trigger if three suggestions were not forthcoming within thirty seconds. The response was a flip chart loaded with great ideas and the birth of my favourite facilitation tool - the 'gun to the head' brainstorm.*

Planning also enables you to establish a timescale for bridging the gap. We have a tendency to over-estimate what we can achieve in shorter timescales (less than a year), and under estimate what could be done in longer ones (over a year). But, the longer range the planning is, the more vulnerable it becomes to uncertainty.

The Path of least resistance

Every change has a path of least resistance. Ask yourself what would be the easiest route to achieve the goal and bridge the gap? It may be simpler than you think.

The event horizon

In all planning there is a limit to how far forward you can predict. Not all of the answers may be available to completely bridge the gap. Accepting this leaves you free to get on with the plan, rather than becoming paralysed. The unknown element is a mini gap, to be managed on the journey and dealt with when better information becomes available.

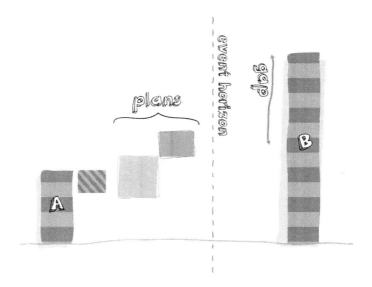

Some ideas require long range planning (major capital investment or new product development), but as a general principle, plan in the SHORTEST TIMEFRAME POSSIBLE.

> *The mobile telecommunications company, at the request of our parent company, embarked on the preparation of a detailed five-year strategy with full financial breakdowns. The work involved months of effort by directors and managers across the whole business. It was packaged and presented, and then eighteen months later, Apple launched the iPhone. The whole game of Mobile Telecommunications changed and the plan was utterly useless. The amount of ink used and the abrasiveness of the paper even made it unsuitable for toilet paper.*

Risk

> *"Everyone has a plan until they get punched in the face" Mike Tyson*

Planning attempts to anticipate future events, but there is always a risk that the plan, or parts of it, may not work. It is also possible that something might happen that disrupts the plan.

Part of the planning and innovation process is to identify these risks. Each risk can be categorized by its significance if it were to happen, and the likelihood of it happening.

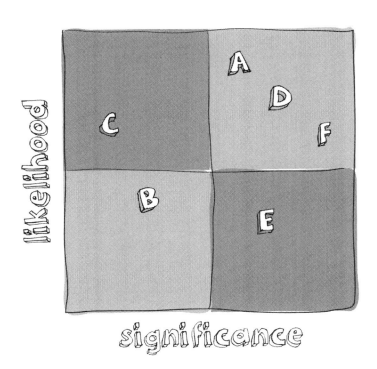

Based on this assessment, decisions can be made as to how the risk will be handled. The choice is to:

- Accept it - acknowledge the risk and to choose not to take any action

- Monitor it- track what is happening to see if the risk is becoming a problem

- Mitigate it - take steps to manage the likelihood or significance of the risk

The awareness and management of risk is a part of any company's day-to-day operations, but is particularly important in times of change.

HABIT TWO - FOCUS

"You can do anything but you can't do everything" - ANON

Focus – The centre of interest or activity. An act of concentrating interest or activity on something.

There are always more things to get done than we ever have time for; an endless list of possibilities, opportunities to be tapped into, problems to be solved, or fun to be had.

Company life is a continuous stream of options, activities, and tasks. Good time management is simply selecting and doing the right ones.

The best time management systems and disciplines in the world will not help you unless you are able to focus on the things that are important.

Learn to say NO. Don't let your mouth put excessive pressure on your back!

Does your daily work routine look like this?

Arrive at work - Step on Hamster wheel and pedal like fury - Leave work.

If your day involves frantically responding to overload, requests, distractions and other peoples problems. If you get home and wonder where the day went and why there is a distinct absence of ticks on your 'to-do' list, then you are stuck on the hamster wheel.

The way to escape the hamster wheel is to allocate some of your time to IMPORTANT stuff, the things you are normally too BUSY to give your attention to. These activities are the normal victims of your 'BUSY-NESS':

- Training, developing and coaching your team

- Upgrading and streamlining systems and processes

- Building connection with customers, colleagues and suppliers

- Looking at internal and market data to make sense of what is going on and how to improve results

- Creating plans of action and coming up with new ideas

- THINKING (when was the last time you put an hour aside to do nothing but THINK?)

Yet the more time you spend working on these things, the more you will notice that all the busy stuff begins to disappear. This is because you are dealing with CAUSES rather than EFFECTS.

Start with an hour a day and make it the first hour of the day. FOCUS on doing one important task before you jump on the hamster wheel.

Focus is about what you are **not** going to **do** as much as what you **are** going to do.

Laser focus

Imagine using a magnifying glass to burn a hole in a piece of paper. If you keep moving the paper and glass around, the heat never builds up enough to ignite the paper. It is only when you bring the light to a fine point, and keep it there, that you generate enough heat to burn a hole.

> *When I worked at a major utility company, we had a problem with late billing. The systems that we had weren't able to produce bills for all customers, and as a result, their bills built up. As a further kick in the pods, the regulator said if we hadn't billed the customer after 12 months, we weren't allowed to bill them.*
>
> *This problem had been going on for a couple of years and it was costing the business money. It had been passed around several senior managers as part of their wider job to resolve it, and none of them had succeeded. If anything, the problem was getting gradually worse and wasn't even on the way to being solved.*
>
> *In the end, it was given to one of my colleagues. He was given it and told that he had six months to fix the problem and he was to do nothing else other than that. Within three months we had no late billing accounts.*

4160

If you live to be 80 you have 4160 weeks in which to achieve all of your dreams and ambitions. Of course you need to subtract the time that has already gone from this

$80 \times 52 = 4160$ - (current age $\times$ 52) = time left

Now think about how well you use your time?

Time is a finite resource and the clock is ticking. Act like it!

> *I have a client in the engineering business. When I first started working with him, he was the only salesperson in the business. He was also the only one who could do electrical wiring. We measured where his time was spent over a period of a couple of weeks and discussed the results.*
>
> *We attached a pound per hour value to each task based on how much he would have to pay for someone else to do that task.*
>
> *He spent some of his time doing some bookkeeping that he could pay someone £30 an hour to do. We also worked out that we could get someone to do electrical wiring for about £55 an hour.*
>
> *The most interesting number was how much he was worth an hour when he was out in front of customers, on average £2,000 of orders an hour.*
>
> *You can probably guess the insight that he had at that moment that changed his habitual behaviours. He still slips back into old habits occasionally, but at least beats himself up about it.*

What could you be doing that is the most valuable use of your time?

Prioritisation is both a challenging and a rewarding discipline. It is not easy to say NO to an idea that makes sense to do. But this is your challenge.

To focus your energy unleashes the very best of you. Focus is not about doing less, it is about achieving more.

If you manage others, you must be prepared to exact the same discipline of focus on what you expect of them as well. Don't overload their backs while trying to free yours.

Five ideas to help you focus

80/20

Pareto's law says that 20% of the effort delivers 80% of the result. It has an uncanny habit of proving itself in all aspects of business.

- 80% of turnover comes from 20% of customers
- 80% of complaints comes from 20% of customers
- 80% of internal problems come from 20% of the team
- 80% of sales come from 20% of products
- 80% of company results come from the efforts of 20% of the team

Are you spending your time focused on the 20%, or wading through the 80%?

The principle of three

Your brain, magnificent though it is, is able to consciously deal with around 3-5 concurrent activities. At a sub conscious level, it can deal with millions of pieces of data a second (you would know if this wasn't true because you would be dead).

By focusing on three things done in any one-day, you will achieve much more.

The board of one of my employers approved a capital expenditure budget for IT and Network system enhancements of £85m. There were 135 projects with a combined cost of £689m bidding for this money. The directors invested (wasted?) an 11-hour board meeting trying to select which of the projects to approve. They still didn't reach a final list that came anywhere near £85m.

I contrast this with another company I worked for where the board approved a capital expenditure budget, but prioritized and allocated the expenditure according to the strategic business needs. As a result, it was not necessary to wade through every project. The decisions on spend within each area were made at

*lower levels of the company. This saved a lot of arguing,
organisational noise, and wasted effort (even if it did annoy a
few people whose projects never got done).*

Juggling too many tasks uses up a lot of energy and time, even just
managing the list!

Decide three priorities and focus relentlessly on them. When they are done
you can pick another three.

The car park

*"More businesses choke on opportunity than
starve of them" - Verne Harnish*

There are always lots of bright, shiny new ideas that you could work on to
improve your company and your life. Ideas are not the challenge,
implementation is. You cannot do everything, so get over it.

They may be good ideas, so make sure they get written down somewhere.
Create an idea car park. It can be a chart on the wall, a white board, a
journal, an excel spreadsheet, a piece of toilet paper. The format is not
important.

The car park has every idea, everything you've got to fix, and every piece of
inspiration that you have had in it. Once an idea is in the car park you can
relax and forget about it. It's not going anywhere.

The car park is a reference source for ideas when the need arises. When
viewed later on, many ideas often don't look as brilliant as they did the first
time round, but for some, the right time will come.

Be a collector of ideas, but a selective implementer.

Fit for purpose

*I did some filming at an aerospace museum and was
particularly struck with their two seat silver Lightning jet that
sat as the gate guardian to the museum. One of the films we
made required me to stand up close to this magnificent cold war*

fighter. Capable of Mach 2 and a ball-breaking rate of vertical climb, it was sleek and perfect - until you got close up.

On close inspection it was full of dents and scratches. There were riveted pieces of metal like silver plasters all over the airframe and it was looking quite sorry for itself. So what! It still did exactly what was required of it.

Taking a look around, I am sure there is a big list of things that need fixing. But remember, a company only needs to be one thing, **fit for purpose**.

Focus on your priorities and use whatever is left over to patch up cracks.

The fit for purpose test - Write a list of everything you think needs to be fixed, and then apply the following scores to each item on your list:

1 - This directly impacts the customer getting the product or service they expected

2 - This impacts company profits because of higher cost or inefficiency

3 - This makes life harder and creates an inconvenience for people in the company

4 - I originally thought this needed fixing, but Dave has changed my mind

Fix the list in the following order - 1, 2, and 3.

The planning dilemma

- Setting priorities over too short a timeframe makes it difficult to focus on significant deliverables.
- Setting priorities over too long a timeframe means that your plans are more likely to become obsolete.

Ninety days (a season or a quarter), is the point of power at which you should make prioritisation decisions. It's a long enough period to get meaningful things done, but short enough to enable recovery of the year if things don't work. Take a day to think, debate, and agree the next 3-5 priorities, and then plan the actions needed to deliver them.

90-day planning steps:

1. Review annual goals and targets

2. Review performance of previous 90-day plan

3. Update your picture of current reality

4. Review feedback and performance indicators

5. Debate and agree no more than 5 key priorities for the next 90-day plan

6. Check the car park for inspiration

7. Plan actions and timescales for the next 90-day period

8. Stop talking and EXECUTE

What if things change?

There is always a chance that a show-stopping event takes priority. If this happens then have the prioritisation debate. Following this simple rule: ONE IN, ONE OUT.

This will force consideration of how important this new priority really is when you are required to STOP something else important.

Decide priorities at the 90-day mark, stop thinking and get doing.

HABIT THREE - ACTION

"Action will remove the doubts that theory cannot solve" - Tehyi Hsieh

Action - A thing done, an act.

How many great plans and ideas never made the leap from paper into actual existence?

It's a big mental leap between decision and action

> *I met up with an entrepreneur in Basingstoke. He was working on building his third business in the IT industry; having already built and sold two eight figure turnover companies.*
>
> *During our meeting, I asked him a question. Most businesses typically get to £1-2 million and then they stop growing. "How did you break past that level?"*
>
> *He told me that he'd been mentored from an early age. The one bit of advice from his mentor, himself a very successful businessman, which had stayed in his mind, was that building a business is like leaping a series of chasms.*
>
> *"When you are running along and you come to a deep, broad chasm, the worst thing you can do is to stop and stare into it".*
>
> *He said, "When I see a big business decision needs to be taken, or changes made, I keep my eyes focused dead ahead and jump. I don't hesitate or slow down or it becomes too scary to make the leap."*

There are four reasons (or excuses) that explain why the chasm between thought and action doesn't always get jumped:

- The reasons to take action are not compelling enough. It can be hard to pay the price if you can't see the promise

- You are not committed enough to the action or the outcome it should produce

- You don't have the skills, resources, tools or time to take action

- The consequences of not taking the action are not bad enough to make you do it

From 'To Do' to 'To Done'

The options for what to do with a day are infinite. You are bombarded with demands from others, emails, texts, Facebook updates, advertisements, ideas, and information. It's a wonder anything actually gets done by anybody, ever.

Making action choices is micro-prioritisation. Every potential task or distraction placed in front of you comes with a standard four-option menu:

- You can **do** the task - If something takes less than seven minutes (BSS) to do, it is better to just do it, as you will lose this amount of time thinking about whether to do it or not anyway

- You can **delay** the task - schedule it to be completed at a further date

- You **don't do** the task – you make the conscious decision not to do it

- You **distribute** the task to someone else (I don't like the word delegate as it implies that you are passing the work to a subordinate. This is not always true).

You cannot avoid the need to **make** a decision and **communicate** it before getting on with your priorities.

When you start, finish

In manufacturing companies, the idea of set up time and cost is well understood. To prepare a production line for a batch of work requires an investment in time that is non-productive. This is for preparing machines, configuring the assembly line, testing, and assembling materials. It is common for the cost per unit to drop as volume increases when you order a run of products from a manufacturer. The set up time has to be absorbed so the more units you produce the lower set up per unit.

The same is true for when you start a task. There is an investment in time as you prepare to do the task. You may have to check correspondence, hold discussions with colleagues, assemble documents and create mental space.

Every time you stop and restart a task you lose time in the shut down and restart. The more distractions and interruptions, the more time you lose.

I reported to a CFO in a utility company and was sat a few desks away from him. This company had followed the seemingly universal fashion that directors should be sat out with their teams, supposedly with their fingers on the pulse.

Every day I watched him fail to stop a barrage of interruptions and conversations with colleagues. I sat near him for almost a year, and in that time I think he was lucky if he got one hour of time that was not disturbed each day.

Kill distractions

One of the audit managers I worked for early in my career had an interesting way of dealing with distractions. He insisted on having an open door policy in his office so that people could ask questions or clear up queries. However, he also had a red baseball hat. If he was wearing the hat he was working on something that required his full attention, and was not to be disturbed. If the hat wasn't on it was fine to interrupt him. It worked, but I was always curious as to why he chose to look ridiculous instead of just closing the door.

Distractions are an abundant resource in the average day. Your family, friends, team, colleagues, boss, customers, and suppliers will assault you with emails, texts, phone calls, social media updates, or sticking their heads round the door.

To get things done needs discipline with you switching off the distractions yourself.

Spend an hour at your desk with the monitor switched off, phone to voicemail, and door shut or go somewhere where you are not being disturbed, and see how much you get done. At the end of the hour, check your emails and phone for messages, deal with them, and then do another hour.

Then try two hours, three hours.

How much did you get done? By the way, it is how I wrote this book.

Distraction destruction is a key task.

Use your diary properly

Most people have access to a diary. We use them to record meetings, dentist appointments and birthdays. This is a criminal misuse of the single most important record in your possession.

Your diary is a pictorial representation of the time you have available.

As soon as you make a decision to take an action, commit the time IN YOUR DIARY. Do not allow it to be replaced with a meeting or an interruption. Imagine that this time was with a major customer. You wouldn't allow that meeting to be interrupted because your 'you've got mail' alarm went off, or a staff member fancied a chat, would you?

Understand your white space ratio

A skill that has to be mastered as you progress through the ranks of a company is how to make choices about your use of time.

If you work in a customer facing, or operations role, you probably need to be able to react to situations as they occur, which requires a higher percentage of 'white space' in your diary (clear time to deal with hamster wheel tasks). People in support function or project roles can live with a lower 'white space' ratio, as immediate demands are less frequent.

Resist the temptation to fill all the gaps in your diary. Keep some 'buffer' time free, because life is a contact sport and shit does indeed happen.

Break stuff down

Some tasks need to be completed over an extended period of time. Some that require resources from other areas of the company become projects. Complex projects can spawn an army of people whose role is purely to co-ordinate the resources and manage the progress of the project.

If a task is too big, we may tend to defer it. For this reason, you should always have a START-line and a DEAD-line for any big task.

Break big activities down into smaller component tasks and schedule these into your diary. Be mindful of your own attention span.

> *Give or take a minute, I can focus on one thing for about an hour before I get bored and distracted. When I have a project, it has to be broken down into one hour chunks. You may have a longer concentration span than me and can break your task down into bigger pieces.*

The best way to split the project down is to copy what an amoeba does. Amoebas reproduce by cell division. They split in two and the two new Amoebas split into two, and so on. Keep dividing the big task until you have chunks that fit your attention span.

Procrastination

In the book 'Eat that Frog', Brian Tracy suggests that the best way to deal with tasks you don't enjoy is to do them first thing and get them out of the way. This clears the task from your mind and it gives you a huge boost for the day.

Thinking about the stuff you are not doing but ought to be doing, is a waste of energy. It creates two destructive thought patterns; guilt (I should have done this) and worry (if I don't do this).

If you find yourself investing in procrastination, break the cycle by doing something else. Better to do something with the time than waste it worrying about what you are not doing.

Just remember, if it's an important task you must GET IT COVERED. Someone has to do it.

When I find my clients procrastinating about a task, it is typically driven by a belief about what they can/can't, do/don't, or will/won't do. It's a grounding issue.

Cashing up

When I worked in retail there were always strict, end of day procedures for balancing and closing cash registers. No one left to go home until the cash balanced with the cash register.

What's your end of day procedure? Do you update your to-do list, spend a few minutes reflecting on what went well and not so well, check your diary and get any documents or information you need ready for tomorrow?

Having an end of day process has huge benefits:

- You can switch off and enjoy your evening

- Your sleep will not be disturbed by panics about where 'that' report is or whether you have your train tickets

- During your sleep, your sub-conscious works on tomorrows agenda and you wake up full of inspiration, ideas and answers

Passing the monkey

One of the partners at the consulting firm I worked in had a unique way of delegating. On his desk he had a jar full of plastic monkeys. Whenever he delegated a task, he gave you a monkey to signify that it was now your job to complete it. He also wrote down whom he had given the monkey to.

His rules were simple. You had to complete the task and return the monkey. It was OK to pass the task on to someone else, provided that they physically accepted the plastic monkey from you. BUT as far as he was concerned, it was your responsibility to make sure it got done.

If you carry any of the following beliefs, you will actively avoid distributing tasks.

"No-one can do the job as well as me"

If this sounds familiar to you, then you are destined for a career on the hamster wheel. If you don't like the sound of that, then take action. Train people to do the job the way you want it done. If they can't, go and find people that can.

"I'm worried they might do the job better than me"

Wouldn't it be an amazing if your team were better than you at doing the job? Think how much time you would have to focus on really important matters if you were free of the hamster wheel.

"I'm in love with fire fighting"

The cut and thrust of daily activity and life on the hamster wheel seems to appeal to some people. The rush they get from fixing problems and playing the hero is like a drug. If this is genuinely what you want your life to be about, then carry on. If at some point you would like to be remembered for making a difference rather than hanging on as tight as you could, then start getting other people to do more stuff.

"I don't want to pay for someone else to do something I can do myself"

Go back and read the 4,160 section, in case you didn't understand it the first time.

Four steps to freedom - how to lose any task

Once you have a defined task, you want someone else to do follow these four steps:

1. Do the task and let the other person watch what you're doing. Get them to ask you questions and involve themselves in what you are doing.
2. Do the task yourself and get the other person to help. Now they are doing something in the task and deepening their knowledge.
3. The other person does the task and you help. You sit there, coach them, and pick up the bits that they are still struggling with.
4. They do the task and you watch. You shut up and let them do it, and then you brief them at the end.

You will have different levels of trust for different employees. Adjust your style and add in more reviews and progress checks when trust is lower.

Mid-course correction

Taking action is what ultimately makes the difference for company and personal success. Not every action and idea you implement will work or have the desired impact. You can never be certain of that. We turn our attention next to how we focus on the impact of the actions taken in order to make mid-course corrections if we are drifting away from our target.

HABIT FOUR - INSIGHT

If I am driving from London to Bristol I can afford to be a few degrees or miles off course. If you have strapped me in a rocket ship and are sending me to Mars, I cannot afford to be even a small percentage of one degree off course. God knows where I will end up. I am relying on you to track my progress and make the necessary mid-course corrections early.

Insight - The capacity to discern the true nature of a situation. The act or outcome of grasping the inward or hidden nature of things, or of perceiving in an intuitive manner.

I cannot remember a single plan of action or strategy that went exactly as planned. There are too many variables. The market changed, a competitor did something unexpected, we couldn't get a process to work, our action had an unforeseen impact, or shit happened somewhere else and scuppered the plan.

Having sufficient early warning systems to tell you when things are changing, or are not working as planned is vital. It allows for rapid corrective action to be taken.

> *One of the directors in the telecommunications company carried a large file around with him wherever he went. It contained operational reports and numbers from the vast and complicated empire that he was responsible for. Whenever he was in board meetings, discussions with his team, or trying to defend his departments from criticism, he would have the facts and statistics to hand. He also expected his team to 'know their numbers' and god help you if you didn't.*

There are two types of information that can be used to understand what is going on;

Quantitative - This is numerical and can be analysed, compared, and modelled, e.g., financial information or operational statistics.

Qualitative - This is not numbers but words, such as customer or employee feedback. It is harder to model and analyse but equally important to use, particularly when repeating themes emerge.

Information overload

Each day you are dealing with lots of data. From financial statements, operating reports, project updates, discussions and meetings, newsletters, notes, emails, the Internet, Skype calls, Facebook, Twitter, YouTube, TV, radio, magazines, newspapers, advertising. Is it any wonder we often feel overwhelmed?

Everyone has a different level of ability to read, interpret, and absorb information. My ex-wife could read a book in a day and then recall details from it five years later. I struggle to remember what I had for breakfast some days.

It is important to filter information before investing in understanding, validating and acting on it. Every piece of information should be handled once, or at most, twice. An initial scan of incoming information can be used to determine which of the four courses of action to take (see the last chapter: Do, Delay, Don't do, or Distribute) There are three ways I get my clients to filter information

- Influence or Control filter - The first acid test is to what extent do you have the ability to take action on the information? If you have an ability to directly control the results, or to wield some influence on them, keep them in your data feed.

- Priority Filter - How important is this information and how directly does it contribute to the achievement of your immediate priorities?

- Exception filtering - Many of the bigger companies I worked for provide summarized information using traffic light statuses. This enables people reading the report to focus their attention where the immediate needs are, rather than having to review everything.

By filtering data you can decide where to focus your attention now. It can be a useful habit to put time aside each week to catch up on 'information' reading.

I was lucky enough to be selected for some free training by the Government last year in recognition of my ability to drive faster than the speed limit. Something I learnt on that fascinating evening was the three sources of decision-making.

- *Fact, i.e., accurate information that we are given*

- *Opinion, our own or someone else's view*

- *Guesswork, our gut feel or best guess at the time*

Be honest with yourself about the basis of the decisions you make. It is important to establish facts where possible. There is inherent risk in opinions or guesswork, although sometimes they are the only option.

Interpreting information

We interpret information differently because we all see the world from our own unique perspective. When looking at information we need to be aware of a number of viruses in the system that can bias our interpretation; particularly these little nasties

The 'Order' virus - Our tendency to try and create structure and meaning even from chaos. Back in the Savannah days we sought to make meaning from the grass swaying in a certain way because it might indicate a Tiger waiting to pounce. When interpreting data, this means we look to establish patterns or meaning. It also means we may ignore the likelihood of random events causing data to fluctuate, particularly when it is a short term observation as opposed to a longer term trend. Ask any politician.

The 'Sense' virus - Information that ties in with how we think the world works is welcomed with open arms into our consciousness. We delight in its honesty and truth. Yet information that does not tie in with our personal map is more likely to be dismissed as erroneous or flawed. Ask any politician.

The 'Right' virus - We love to be right. We don't like to think of ourselves as liars so when we are presented with information, we have a remarkable ability to distort it so it fits with the truth that we need to hear. Ask any politician.

The 'Anecdotal Extrapolation' virus - I have noticed a tendency amongst my clients for taking a single problem, or failure, and extrapolating it into a crisis of business destroying magnitude. Ask any politician.

From time to time we are given information or we see something differently and the light bulb goes off in our head. The light bulb offers us fresh perspective or a new idea that we hadn't previously thought of. We should trust these moments, but check for viruses.

The five key sensors

Human beings have five primary senses: sight, sound, touch, taste, and smell. These are the sensors that provide our brains with information about what is going on in the world. A company has five sensors:

- Customers – Connections with customers enable you to sense what is going on in the market so you can react to changes

- Employees – People in your organisation who are operating the business are a direct sensor for what is and isn't working

- Suppliers – Suppliers can be a valuable source of information about what is happening in the wider industry

- Financial Information – The scoreboard for the game of business is the financial data. Financial data tends to be after the event, but still vital

- Operational Information – Information about customer and operational activities

  One of my clients had a real challenge with getting his team talking to customers. His team consisted, in the main, of introvert and task focused people. They were not particularly communicative.

  He set a goal that at his Friday afternoon team meeting, every member of staff had to bring five pieces of information that they learnt from talking to customers each week.

  At first they really squirmed and didn't like the goal; they found all manner of excuses, but after a while, some interesting information started to permeate through.

  They started to get opportunities to quote for more business. In one conversation with a client, their contact said, "Oh I'm just off to go and take a look at this job up in Leeds." As a result of this short sentence they picked up an opportunity to quote for a high value piece of work.

What's on your dashboard?

My car has two key information sensors, the dashboard and the satellite navigation. The dashboard tells me at any point in time how fast I am travelling, how hard the engine is working, how much fuel I have, and whether the car is operating correctly. The satellite navigation tells me the progress towards my end goal, whether I am on/off course and where the speed cameras and traffic jams are.

What's the dashboard for your part of the company? What are the key indicators that tell you whether your area/department is performing as expected? How regularly do you receive this information and is it quick enough for you to be able to act on (it helps to know about a speed camera before you drive through it)?

Are you accessing information from all five sensors, and if not, what information would you ideally have? It's just as important to understand what information you are not receiving (your blind spots).

Remember:

"Ignorance is not bliss. Ignorance is ignorance. It is not right to believe anything can be derived from it" Sigmund Freud

Good information enables you to see beyond the now, see deeper into a situation, and take corrective action. The faster the market is changing, the faster you need to be able to produce/report information.

The more times you review and explore information the better you get at spotting issues.

One of my team came to see me with a look of complete panic on her face. We had posted some key numbers into the company's Profit and Loss account and the information had gone to the main board. She had identified a problem with the data resulting in a material misstatement of some of our revenue.

As she struggled for breath and spurted out the information to me something was not stacking up in my head. I had been talked through some of the numbers and the associated data. What she was saying didn't make sense.

Rather than panic and join her in her meltdown, potentially wasting hours of my time, I calmly told her to go away, take a look at the issue she had identified and come back in 24 hours if there was still a problem.

The next day she came back having found an error in her spreadsheet.

Understanding numbers

As an auditor I have learnt to be deeply suspicious of information provided to me, especially when it comes from a source I don't understand. I have a mental checklist I go through when presented with numbers.

- Is this information accurate? Can I rely on the source of this information and is there other data available that supports it?

- Is it complete? Have I been given all of the information or only part?

- Is this information timely? Do I understand what time period this information relates to and how up to date this is?

- How big is this? When I look at a number, e.g., number of customer complaints, the data needs to be compared to the total population, e.g., total number of orders

- Compared to what? Data on its own is seldom very useful, it comes alive when it's compared to similar data, for example, sales against budget or sales compared to a similar period. This gives me a sense of the relative importance of the information and whether it is good or bad news

Into the unknown

When a company wants to do something new there may be little or no information as to whether it will be a success or not. This is part of the game of managing risk. Without taking risks a company can never grow.

One way of reducing risk is to conduct small-scale experiments with new ideas, the results of which can be measured before a wider role out. For example, you might pilot a new type of bakery layout in a superstore and measure the difference it creates before upgrading all four hundred stores.

Using the information gleaned from testing and measuring approaches can be a valuable source of what to focus on in the next planning cycle.

The pace of change means that you should be spending proportionately more time trying to understand the present and less trying to predict an ever-uncertain future.

> *I spent some time talking to an analyst in the energy company I worked for. His job was to forecast future gas demand in the industry. I asked him about global warming and what evidence he had seen to confirm or refute the hypothesis.*
>
> *He told me that gas demand forecasting used to be done with a 71-year time series of data. About ten years ago they realized that this was providing very unreliable demand projections. After analysis they moved to a 17-year time series of data. A few years later they realized this was not providing accurate results and so moved to a 5-year time series.*

Is your company still basing assumptions about the future on a past that no longer has ANY relevance?

Final thoughts on execution

If every business consisted of one person and required no interaction with other people, individuals would need no to do nothing more than consistently execute against the four habits of intent, focus, insight, and action.

Of course it doesn't work that way in any aspect of business or life. Any commercial endeavour requires interaction with other people. They are customers, suppliers, intermediaries, and colleagues.

Our ability to connect effectively with others is THE most important ability to master in business.

CONNECTION

When two people comfortable in their own skin, devoid of ego and judgment of each other, meet and talk, a true connection is established, and things change.

Have you ever had that experience of a deep connection with someone? Something that goes beyond the words they are saying. It's a felt experience as well as an exchange of words.

We think of this as an exception to the rule. WRONG! It's our default setting.

Human beings are wired to connect to each other at a deep level. The connection breaks down when we have pre-conceptions about the other person or the conversation.

The ability to connect is THE SINGLE MOST IMPORTANT BUSINESS AND LIFE SKILL you possess.

If computers ran businesses, they would follow the commercial principles adjusting to meet the market demand and supply. It is the introduction of people into the business world that creates all the confusion and excitement. People operate to a set of principles as well, but these principles result in every one of us seeing the world through our own unique perspective.

It is the infinite complexity of emotions, reactions, and behaviours that create the fun and frustrations of business life. There are also the added complications of the different types of relationships that exist between colleagues, departments, customers, suppliers, shareholders, stakeholders, and competitors.

Our brains limit the number of strong relationships we can have to less than fifty. This is connected to the typical tribe size that existed during the most significant periods of history for our brains development.

With today's large organizations and the explosion of connection technologies, it is no surprise that we can under-invest in important connections with people in our workplace.

It is not uncommon to be expected to have a working relationship with people you have never met over poor communication channels, like email, it is easy to see how 'getting the wrong end of the stick' becomes a day-to-day occupational hazard.

In the absence of a deep connection with people, we often believe that we are mind readers. We react to communications as though we know what the other person is thinking. The limited information we have enables space for our wonderfully creative minds to think up all sorts of motives for their odd or frustrating behaviour.

There is an underlying principle that can help us interpret and understand each other's behaviour better. I call it the principle of **Positive intent.**

No one takes any action or decision that they don't believe has a positive intention at the time they take it. Even people that commit atrocities believe that they were doing the right thing in that moment. To code-break anyone's motives requires that you first seek to understand the intentions behind their actions.

This needs just three simple (yet for difficult to apply) skills:

- the shutting of one's own cake hole

- asking good questions

- listening to the answers

I do not have enough digits on my body to count the number of times where the application of one or more of these skills would have resulted in better outcomes in my own career, and those of others.

> *One evening whilst working late in the office, a manager from another department dropped in to see me. Before I'd even put my pen down, she launched into a tirade of abuse about one of my team who was not 'following process'. She told me that I had to resolve this issue immediately. I paused and turned to face her, my mind racing for the answers, which I didn't have. In the end I calmly said to her, "I don't know who the hell you think you are, coming over and shouting at me this time of night, but I suggest you go away and make an appointment to see me in the morning when you are prepared to be a little more polite." She stormed off clearly furious at the lack of commitment from me.*

> *In order to give her a proper response, I would have had to speak to my line manager so I could understand the process and figure out a plan to resolve the issue, and that was not going to happen at 7pm. She had not attempted to understand how aware or not I was of the situation, or even spoken to the person concerned directly. She backed herself into a communication hole.*

> *There was an additional piece of information that would have been useful for her to know before embarking on her assault. A week later it was to be announced that I was taking over her department and that she would be reporting to me. Do you think life might have played out differently for her if she had*

taken more time to connect before expressing an opinion?

"Seek first to understand and then to be understood" - Steven Covey

These words changed my life. Instead of arguing and trying to convince people that you are right, it is far more useful to invest time in understanding the other person's points of view. When I remember to do this, a solution always gets found that both parties are committed to, in far less time.

Curiosity is the new intellect

"In times of rapid change, experience could be your worst enemy" Jean Paul Getty

Whatever expertise you have is based on the experiences and knowledge you have built up. It is historic. These days, things change fast. Business models and knowledge can become out-dated almost overnight.

We need new information. We can open up the possibility of getting it by becoming more curious.

> *I went to meet an Indian business owner who ran a successful aromatherapy and perfumery business. Other coaches had told me that Indian business owners are particularly difficult clients to attract and tend to resist the idea that they could improve on what they are doing. This was not a healthy idea to walk into a sales meeting with.*

> *The meeting was a battle from the start. I did everything wrong. I tried every angle to find areas where he would express an interest in help, and he just kept quiet or defended the way he did things. After an hour of trying (at one point we were practically shouting at each other) I sat back in my seat. As I looked around I noticed all the bottles arranged in cabinets in his office. It dawned on me that I had no idea how perfume was made, so I asked him to show me.*

*He took me down to the lab and excitedly showed me around,
and I learnt a whole bunch of information that if I had
bothered to ask up front, would have changed everything. I
didn't leave with a client, but I left with two bottles of perfume,
a slice of cherry pie that his wife had made, and a friend.*

Being curious is not as simple as we would like it to be. When we receive information we weigh it on our mental scales, comparing it to our existing knowledge and our model of how we think the world is.

If it doesn't fit our view, we challenge it or reject it. How many new, exciting and radical ideas failed to get past these filters?

If it does fit, we either use it, or pat ourselves on the back for being so clever and ignore it, because we already knew it.

If you try being curious and eager to learn you will hear lots of new information, even in things you already 'knew'. Not only that, but others love to explain things. You will find people like you and give you more information, because you have connected with them.

Suspend personal judgement on any information you receive. Instead immediately jump in with 'how could I use this?' or 'how good am I at this?'

Questions are the answer

*"I keep six honest serving-men, (they taught me
all I knew); Their names are What and Why
and When and How and Where and Who."*
Rudyard Kipling

As an auditor I learnt to ask questions, lots of questions. Just when you thought you'd answered everything, I kept digging deeper. Like Columbo, I always had 'one more question'. This is because I am lazy. The more questions I asked, the easier my job was as I could spend less time doing boring work like testing and reconciliations. This saved me a lot of time, kept my job interesting, and kept me in flow.

There is no greater compliment in life than someone saying, 'that's a great question'. That's when you know you are connecting at a deeper level and inviting them to explore something completely new for them.

My friend, Jennifer, asks everyone she meets these questions (she adapted from Malcolm Gladwell's book, 'The Tipping Point'):

- What do you do?

- What are you great at?

- What are you passionate about?

These three questions seem to spark something in anyone who is asked them.

By using more questions and talking less, you get lots of new information and create deeper connection with people.

Mining with questions

By structuring questions into layers, you can quickly get to the bottom of whatever you are trying to figure out. In your next conversation, try to follow this order:

- Ask an open question (one that can't be answered with a yes or no answer) to get the person talking

- Ask probing questions to get to the juicy detail

- Ask clarifying questions to confirm things you are not quite clear on

- Ask evidential questions to find information that supports what you are learning

- Repeat what you heard them say (to show you are listening and to give them a chance to correct any misunderstanding)

- Always ask the big AE - Anything Else? Once someone is in flow they may think of other relevant points to tell you about.

Don't bottle the big question

Don't interrogate, but don't be afraid to ask questions, particularly the challenging questions (the ones that frighten you a bit when you think about asking them). Just explain why you are asking a difficult question before you ask it, particularly if it is making you nervous.

I went to meet a business owner to talk about coaching. He was really resisting telling me about his business, which had been running for about seven years, and didn't seem ready or open to conversation about paying me money to help him. I tried everything, profitability, his involvement in the business, what strategies he had tried, etc. etc. It was a tough gig, he was giving me nothing. He could tell I was asking questions as a way of trying to sell him coaching. He was not going to be that easily fooled. Towards the end of our session, I asked him what he did before he set the business up. It turned out that he had been a Weapons Inspector in Iraq. I was fascinated and asked him lots of questions from a place of genuine curiosity, including the obvious one. By the time we finished, he had become really friendly and engaged with me.

If I had approached our initial conversation with the same degree of excitement and interest, I suspect we would have worked together and had a great time transforming his business.

Decide that you will get to know everyone you talk to a little bit more than you know them now.

These are not the answers I was looking for

Make sure you get the answer to the question that you asked, and not some rambling diatribe.

One of my clients agreed to make 50 sales phone calls a week to his existing customers. The following week I asked him this question:

ME: So how many calls did you make last week?

He began to explain to me how busy he had been and that there had been a crisis in the business that consumed a lot of his time.

ME: So how many calls did you make last week?

He explained that he had prepared to make the calls on Tuesday morning, but he got distracted by a customer enquiry.

ME: So how many calls did you make last week?

He showed me the schedule of planned calls and went on that he thought next week would be a lot easier.

I got a piece of paper from my folder and drew a square on it before handing it over to him

ME: Please write in the box the number of calls you made last week!

The dumbest question on the planet is always the one you didn't ask

When you were a kid I bet you asked lots of questions. In fact, I bet your parents got fed up with it. As we grow up, we become more self-aware and afraid of asking a dumb question that could embarrass us in front of our classmates and colleagues. We would rather balls something up than ask a question that risks us looking dumb. What is the question asking culture in your company? Is it 'if you don't know, ask', or 'if you don't know keep your head down and pretend you do'?

We don't like being rejected or judged by others. This used to be a very useful tool for us. If we upset anyone we risked getting kicked out of our tribe, which meant almost certain death in the wilderness. Society has outpaced the brains evolution.

We still try to avoid rejection, even though it carries no impact to us (there are no Tigers in the shopping mall) and is also unlikely to create the response in others that we expect. More often than not, when you do ask the 'dumb' question in a room full of people, everyone else breathes a sigh of relief because they wanted the answer too.

There is nothing to lose, but everything to gain by asking questions.

Listening

Asking brilliant questions is of little use if you are not listening to the answers. Listening well is a dying skill. We are so bombarded with sound bite messages that we are losing the ability to remain focused for more than a few seconds on a message.

We all have ADHD.

Even when we 'listen intently' we are often doing it in order to think up something clever to say next.

Effective listening requires that you have NOTHING on your mind. Listening to someone like you would listen to music allows the messages beyond people's words to impact you.

Our words convey a very small percentage of any messages. Research suggests as little as 7% (BSS) of language is words, 38% is in the tone, and the balance comes from body language and facial expressions. A large part of any message is picked up and interpreted subconsciously. If you are not concentrating on the person, you can lose a lot of the message.

> *"The most important thing in communication is*
> *to hear what isn't being said" — Peter Drucker*

Pay attention to what people are NOT saying, as much as what they are. There is value in the spaces!

When you really listen to somebody with nothing on your mind, there is a feeling behind the words that you can tune into. This is the place where connection happens. In this connection, relationships become truly effective and problems get effortlessly solved.

Listen with NOTHING on your mind when someone is talking to you.

Pick the channel

When you have something of importance to say, it pays to think about how you deliver your message. Painting a heart on a stone and lobbing it through your lovers window is seldom received as an act of love. The way a message is delivered is as important as the content.

The default should be verbal, and ideally, face to face. Remember emails, letters, text messages, and social media messages seldom communicate the full emotion of what you are trying to say. I never use email as a tool of first contact with anyone I don't know, simply because my goal is to create a connection with them.

Emailing does not remove the obligation to follow up. Before you send an email, ask 'am I sending this to help the other person, or to protect me?'

Most people have to manage a large volume of electronic messages. Don't assume that because you have sent a message to someone that they have read, taken action, or accepted responsibility to do what you have asked. It is your bad manners to assume they have.

If in doubt; PICK UP THE PHONE.

Brevity

When it is your turn to speak, there are some simple principles worth remembering that can support your message.

- Use as few words as possible to convey your message. This should stop you from boring the pants off 75% of your listeners. Be brief and invite questions instead

- Test the other persons understanding of what you have told them. You are responsible for your communication. If you don't get the desired result, the chances are your message was wrong

- Always strive to create a win-win outcome in any discussion. Winning the debate may make you feel good in the short term, but in the long term strong relationships are more important

- Use lots of stories in your communications. Information has been passed from generation to generation through the use of stories, and they are still the most effective way of explaining or teaching something

- If in doubt, stop and ask yourself W.A.I.T. - Why Am I Talking?

Your network

Who are the people you need to be in regular contact with? How frequently do you need to connect with them and does this need to be on a 1-1 basis, or a 1-many basis?

Who is in your inner circle (direct reports, key customers, boss, and other key departments)? How often should you, and do you, connect with them, and by what means?

type	name	freq	method
supplier	paul:sleeping tiger	monthly	email
customer	janet p	quarterly	phone
customer	robert j	monthly	phone + email
internal	john (accts)	monthly	drop in
internal	richard (boss)	weekly	face 2 face
		daily	phone

Transactional vs. Relationship connections

I get my clients to draw up a communications plan for their customers. It is easy to get sloppy with connections and end up only ever speaking to people when you need something done, or need an answer.

This sorts out a problem, but it does NOT develop a relationship. Make sure you put time aside regularly to connect with your network, purely to connect and understand what's going on.

Be proactive in your relationships, not transactional.

Managing your meetings

Meetings have a bad reputation. The reason for this is that many of them are a waste of time. How many times have you sat bored in a room, thinking that you have just spent two hours of your life that you will never get back?

When you choose to bring a group of people together to make a connection (i.e., a meeting), there are some simple rules that can ensure no one's time gets wasted and that there is real value in the time that's spent.

- Have an agenda and timings, and stick to them no matter what

- Make sure the purpose of the meeting is clear. Are you just communicating news, asking for decisions, or exploring options? If it's all one-way traffic communication, do you really need a meeting?

- Only have things on the agenda that are relevant to everyone in the room and that they are able to contribute to. RESPECT their time as well as yours

- Stop anyone from hogging the microphone. Stop the bore before everyone loses the will to live

- Open every meeting by going around the table and giving everyone a timed minute to update people with what is going on for them. It helps everyone understand each other and gets issues out in the open

- Agree actions and record them in the meeting, not five days afterwards

- Don't use the standard hour. Have more 20-minute meetings. Try having meetings without seats and see how efficient everyone becomes with communication

- Make people contribute by going around the table and asking everyone for ideas and thoughts. Even better, have different people facilitate different sections of the meeting

- Start and finish on time, whether everyone is there or not. Do not waste people's time sitting around

- For regular monthly departmental meetings, use a standard agenda and get different people to run different sections

- Take responsibility for the energy in the meeting. If people aren't participating, that is your problem, not theirs

When I took my first role as head of an audit team, they held weekly meetings on a Monday morning at 10am. After an extended pre-amble, while everyone made coffee and talked about their weekends, at some point the session would start. These meetings consisted of each person updating on the status of the project they were working on and explaining (frequently in tedious detail) what was holding it up. Others would then chip in with their experiences, offer advice, and take pot shots at each other to make their own lack lustre performance look better. At the end of the meeting there were never any agreed actions, and after attending a few, I also realized I was no clearer about progress against targets than when we started.

I changed the agenda. I made the meeting start at 9am, and I mean start. We would then look at NUMBERS. Specifically, we would review project progress against milestones and budgets. There would only be a discussion on actions to take if any project was not on track.

We then went around the table and each team member was asked to raise any issues or challenges they were having, and to also outline exactly what they were going to be doing in the coming week. We didn't get into solving any of the issues, but took actions for people to speak outside the meeting, thereby avoiding everyone having to sit around listening to things of no consequence to them.

Finally, I would wrap up the session with any news or updates I had for the team. Forty minutes later - JOB DONE!

Welcome feedback

Anyone who cares about performance encourages feedback. It is the breakfast of champions. They see no reason to shy away from it, irrespective of its source. All feedback is an opportunity to further improve in pursuit of what they want.

YOUR REACTION TO ANY COMMUNICATION IS A REFLECTION OF YOURSELF, NOT THE OTHER PERSON.

Final thoughts on connection

The skills of connection are not exclusive to the workplace. Take the opportunity to develop deep connections with everyone you meet. These connections create trust, and when people trust you, they open their networks to you. Who knows where that may lead you?

Building connections enables your own influence to extend and grow. There is supposedly only six degrees of separation between you and anyone else on the planet (research by Facebook in 2011 showed an average degree of separation of 4.74 amongst its massive global community), so connections can take you a long way towards achieving your goals.

Your ability to connect, persuade, and influence people is impacted by how grounded you are. We have all had experiences of people who say one thing and appear to do another, who we have nagging doubts about.

In the next section we go inside of you, the individual, to uncover the ultimate leverage point that controls your success or performance in any endeavour; your own personal grounding.

GROUNDING

*"Don't ask what the world needs. Ask what
makes you come alive, and go do it. Because what
the world needs is people who have come alive"* -
Howard Thurman

The best you

Some days nothing seems to go right and you get nothing done. This leaves
you stressed, anxious and annoyed with yourself. They suck.

Other days you seem to show up at your absolute best; confident, focused,
and motivated. You get loads done, and yet it doesn't feel like hard work.
What is that about?

Then in between these opposites are the hundreds of average days you
have.

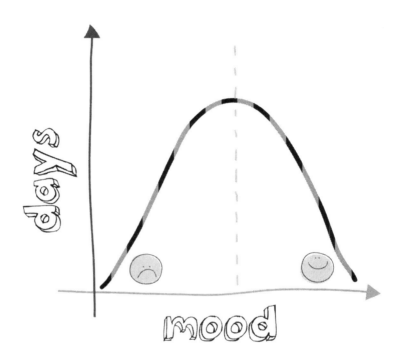

There is a best you, and that is the one you should focus on. It is where your 'A' game shows up.

Wellbeing as a default

The best you is not the result of the odd fluky day. It is your default setting. This is you when you are GROUNDED. Our default is to have wellbeing, feel productive, and be happy. Whenever we feel anxious or stressed, we have moved away from our default. All you need to figure out is how the system works and where the reset button is. So how do you access this mythical genius inside of you?

The myth of positive mind-set

Before you reach for the sick bag, let me be clear about something. The best you does not get accessed by working on your positive mind-set.

My experience of life is the same as yours is. Some days I am feeling full of wonder and possibility, other days I feel crap and everything sucks. I haven't found a secret happy pill that leaves me permanently in a state of joy and happiness. Can you imagine how annoying I would be if I had, and how much you would want to punch me in the face?

The difference is that I recognize that my default is wellbeing and I know where my experiences, good and bad, are coming from. Understanding how the system works helps me to cope with whatever is going on in any particular moment.

DO NOT TAMPER WITH YOUR MIND-SET, IT IS A SELF-CORRECTING SYSTEM.

Finding your grounding is reliant on your ability to be honest with yourself. Trying to convince yourself that everything is great when you have just stubbed your toe on the bed, missed your train and spilt coffee down your freshly dry cleaned suit, will make you question your own thinking. How much trust will you put in your judgement when you need it to be reliable and truthful?

Four key questions

The best you is confident, clear about what you want, willing to do what it takes, and connects effortlessly with others. When you are grounded life is not a battle to be won, but an adventure to be enjoyed.

I have found four questions really valuable for people trying to access their most irritatingly wonderful 'best self':

1. How does the world work?

2. Who am I?

3. What do I want?

4. How do I show up?

The challenge is that the real answers are not what you think they are.

How does the world work?

The Fundamental Misunderstanding

Your brain processes millions of pieces of data each second to create the experience you have of life. This happens at both a conscious and subconscious level. The vast majority is at the subconscious level, so you don't even know that it's happening. You construct 100% of your experience of life inside your head! You make it all up.

As you go about your daily life you have good and bad days. It looks like the things that happen to you give rise to good and bad feelings. On days when you feel good, it is because good things are happening, and vice versa, when the boss has given you a rollicking, you think that is why you feel stressed.

WRONG!

Your feelings never come from what is happening outside. The feelings of happiness, unease, anxiety, and stress are not coming from the events. They are indicators of the quality and reliability of what I going on in your head. High quality and reliable thinking comes with feelings of wellbeing, calm, and joy. Low-grade thinking comes with feelings of unease, stress, and anxiety.

> *I noticed in the last few years of my corporate career I would get feelings of stress and anxiety about my workload. I put this down to my boss placing unreasonable demands and deadlines on me. Several of my colleagues complained of the same challenges and we would sit over lunch bemoaning our workload. We used to conspire in each other's misery, all of us except one. He had the same workload as the rest of us, but he seemed to effortlessly carry on calmly and without complaint. The only difference between us was that his thinking about*

workload was different to mine.

You are as busy as you think you are remains the quote that angers more of my clients than anything else I say.

You only ever feel 'thinking', not events and circumstances. Even when it really looks like it, it's still an inside-out model.

The death of positive mind-set

Realising that your thinking is not real frees you to choose to act on, or ignore it. As you notice how it changes from moment to moment you can see that it naturally self corrects, provided you are willing to stop tinkering around with it. Faking a positive mind-set actually interferes with the system.

A steady stream of thought flows in and out of your consciousness. You can only have one thought in your conscious mind at any one time. If you think you hate being in a traffic jam, that thought occupies your mind until another one replaces it. If you try and analyse why the traffic is slow, or even worse, try and think what a positive experience the jam is, you keep your attention on it and get even more annoyed.

Once something occurs to you, you can't un-think it. It is too late. Let it go and it will get replaced. Stress and anxiety are born out of believing that what is in your head is important.

High-quality thinking accesses a deeper level of wisdom from inside you; your intuition and common sense are available to you.

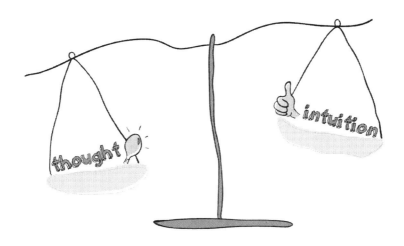

When your head is all revved up and overwhelm is creeping in, the best thing you can do is go and do something different or take time out. Here is my list of four things that work for me:

- Learning - Pick up a book and read about something you don't understand or have current knowledge of. Just taking in new information can settle a fogged up mind

- Exercise - Giving your body a workout also relaxes your mind

- Connecting - Spend time with people talking and exchanging ideas can reset your system, especially if you have been working alone for a while

- Go for a walk in the countryside or outdoors.

Everyone has something that can reset their thinking.

FIND YOUR OWN RESET BUTTON.

Who am I?

"Today you are you, that is truer than true.
There is no one alive who is youer than You." -
Dr Zeus

I was taught a simple success formula in coach training.

Be x Do = Have

To have whatever you want means working on the person you are (be), and the actions you take (do). As a coach, I helped clients upgrade their mindset, develop new skills, take on new knowledge, and take the actions they needed to, in order to get what they *thought* they wanted. It was sometimes hard work to get them where they wanted to go, until I realized that the model is fundamentally wrong. You do not need to change or improve yourself in order to have what you want. In fact, it is the complete opposite of how it really works.

So I changed it to this:

Authentic Self x Action = what you truly want

Not as succinct I admit, but far more accurate.

The diamond, the horseshit, and the nail varnish

Michael Neill, one of my favourite coaches and authors, uses this metaphor for the human condition.

You were born perfect, like a diamond. You had no sense of who you were, what was right, and what was wrong. Your instincts guided you in the moment and your body was kept healthy and safe by processes that you were, and still are, unconscious of.

Just like an acorn contains everything required to create an oak tree, you contain everything you need to become **the authentic you.** You did not need a coach, a therapist, a counsellor, or a book. Your inner guidance system allowed you to get on with stuff. When you were hungry or smelly you cried out. The rest of the time you just hung out, had fun, and slowly took in all that you needed to know. You were virtually fearless. If I put a Tiger in the room you would not be afraid, just cautious. In fact, you were only frightened of two things, falling and loud noises.

You were completely present to what was happening, watching, listening, feeling, and taking it all in.

As your senses and communication abilities grew, you started to design your personal map of the world, your understanding of how things worked, and how you fitted into it.

By the time you were seven, all of the input from parents, teachers, friends, and your own experiments had created most of your map of how things are. You changed from being you and started to become **who you think you are.** You covered the diamond in horseshit.

You took these beliefs into the workplace. Then, as your career developed, you became aware that **who you think you are** was not always how you wanted other people to see you. So what did you do?

You put a coating of nail varnish over the horse shit by starting to pretend to be what you thought people wanted you to be. You tried to become **who you want people to think you are**.

Underneath all of these layers sits the best you; the grounded you, hidden from the world and yourself.

What are the horseshit and the nail varnish?

Your words and actions don't give other people a full or accurate picture of you. Under the surface you have a mountain of thinking that shapes your responses, decisions, and actions in the moment. This is based on who you think you are, how you fit into the world, and how the world works.

This thinking can be a positive force, or it can put the brakes on your performance. It tries to keep us safe by trying to keep us in familiar territory.

You love familiarity. The love of familiarity, and suspicion of the unfamiliar, was pretty useful at one point in human evolution. It might stop you going over to investigate a strange shape in the bushes that could be a Tiger.

These days, this in-built desire for familiarity creates comfort zones and stops us from extending to the full reach of our capabilities. We even call them comfort zones as though they are real.

THE COMFORT ZONE IS A CREATION OF YOUR THINKING. THEY DO NOT, AND HAVE NEVER, EXISTED OUTSIDE YOUR HEAD.

"Everything you could ever want is there. Just outside your comfort zone" - James Allen

Whenever you cross through a comfort zone (bungee jumping, public speaking, roller coasters, drinking a sour shot, you know the stuff) you find that there was actually nothing to be afraid of, and if anything, you want another go.

We imagine that something is going to be terrible or bad for us before we have even tried it.

This imagination also informs you about:

- who you are and who you're not
- what you are scared of and fearless of
- what you are good at and not good at
- what you should and shouldn't do
- what you could and couldn't do

Belief in any of this will tend to let you settle for, at best, average performance and an average life. You will argue for your limitations. Highly successful people still have this stuff going on, but there is one subtle difference for them.

THEY DONT BELIEVE IT.

> *"Whether you think you can or you think you can't, you're right" - Henry Ford*

Much of the horseshit is hard wired in your brains neural pathways giving you the strong illusion that it is reality.

Here is the real truth:

You can do so much more than you think you can and so much more than the very best 'you' that you could imagine, thinks you can.

> *For years in the world of weightlifting, there was a long held belief that a human being could not lift more than 500lb., eventually a weight lifter was tricked into lifting 501.5lbs when the scales were rigged. Once one person had done it others soon followed. It was a thought created barrier.*

What are your self-imposed performance barriers?

The nail varnish represents attempts to improve yourself (remember you are already perfect). Copying others, self-development, doing what you think other people want rather than what you believe to be right, and pretending to be feeling or doing things you are not; these are layers of nail varnish.

Useful ideas can come from learning and applying other people's suggestions, but you should first and foremost learn to trust yourself and do what feels right for you.

Your story

When you look back over your life and career, what is the story you tell yourself? Your story informs your thinking and has a huge impact on the decisions you make and the actions that you take, in your job and life.

I used to tell myself a story of how lucky I had been in my career and how I wasn't good enough to have achieved the success I did. I made it all up and did a very thorough job of it. So good in fact that it felt real enough for me to behave like it was true for much of my career.

I felt particularly strongly that I wasn't as clever as everyone around me, because I didn't have a degree and hadn't come through a graduate programme. Then someone showed me that it was possible to re-write my story. My mentor got me to tell my life story as though everything that had ever happened to me happened with only one intention: **to get me exactly where I was now.**

None of the facts of the story changed, yet everything changed. Instead of being 'lucky' and not really having a credible career, I saw how I had actually done incredible things, fought against the odds, and acquired an unparalleled understanding of how businesses and people work. The crap stuff, whilst tough to deal with at the time, had shaped me in positive ways. It had tuned my skills of connection, helped me cope with challenges, and given me the occasional convenient reminder of my own mortality. Everything that happened got me here.

My understanding of myself, and my honesty with myself, gives me a strong grounding from which I can operate.

The story you tell yourself about yourself is just a story. You are not even a reliable teller of your own story, and in any case, it is not real. It is your best guess of the version of events that have happened to you. Others will see your story differently and more often than not, will think much more highly of you than you do of yourself.

What do you want?

"No-one told him it was impossible so he went and did it" - Unknown

You can choose what you want to achieve and have in your life. This is a unique choice in nature. As far as I am aware, a tree's lifestyle options are relatively limited. When did you last sit down and ask:

"What do I really want from my life and my work?"

The downside of this choice is that you can get confused, or lose focus on what you really want. You can easily fall into the trap of believing that you want what other people tell you that you want.

From an early age, we get told what we should want:

- Parents have their dreams and expectations for us, based on their understanding of what happiness and success is

- Marketing companies bombard us with images of what a perfect body, house, and life is supposed to look like

- Education stifles our individuality and creativity. My careers teacher told me, "Don't be stupid lad" when I told him I wanted to be a fighter pilot. He gave me a bunch of apprenticeship brochures to read

- We are taught to believe that money and status are important markers in society, to the point that some people are willing to defer their happiness until they get enough of them.

Seeing past all of this noise, particularly the idea that money and status are important, can be difficult. This conditioning runs deep.

Here's a good question to start the process off:

What would you do for a living if every job paid the same?

I got talking to a fellow motorcyclist in a café in Salisbury. I had been following him for a few miles across Salisbury plain. It turned out he lived two miles up the road from me. I asked him what he did for a living and he told me he was a dustman. "Do you enjoy it?" I asked. He told me he loved his job. I wasn't expecting this answer so I asked what it was about the job he loved. He enjoyed the early starts, the physical work, and the banter with his crew. He added that he enjoyed doing the little extras for people, particularly the pensioners on his rounds, but the targets they were now under made it impossible to complete a normal round, let alone help anyone.

When you take money and ego out of the equation, we all just love to do what we love to do. This opens up a great deal of choice that we may have been blind to.

Your current job

Think about your current role. What do you love about it, what do you really not like about it, and what are you indifferent to? Are you in the right job, and if not, what would the right job look like? How could you organise your job around the things that you like? What would need to change **in you** to enjoy your job more? A company will always be best served by employees who enjoy their jobs and your life is best served by a job you enjoy doing. I have a long held suspicion that most people end up in a job that, at some level, they enjoy.

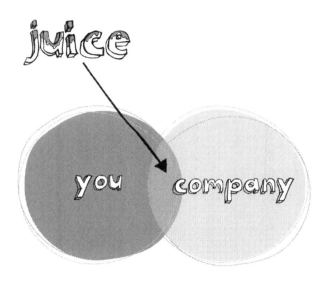

The idea of flow

There are some things that you really love doing. These activities put you in a state of flow. Flow happens when you enjoy what you are doing so much that you lose track of time. In many cases the work comes so naturally to you that it feels effortless. For this reason you don't often realize what your true flow activities and skills are. It can pay to ask other people what you are good at in order to get some insight.

Once you understand the activities that put you in flow, you can focus on creating more opportunities to do that kind of work.

> *"If you find a job you really love, you'll never work again" – Winston Churchill*

Start where you are

> *I was on a flight to Spain. The flight was full of mechanics from a number of Formula One teams heading out for testing in Jerez. I love motor racing and was delighted as two of them sat*

next to me on the flight. I was looking forward to finding out just how exciting it must be to be involved in the world of F1. They spent the whole two hour flight whining about the hours they had to work, the time spent away from home and that some of the other teams got paid more than them and had better expense policies!

The grass may look greener on the other side, but that is because it is largely fertilized with bullshit. What other people do just LOOKS better. That does not mean it is better.

"There is not better than here. There is just different to here" – Michael Neill

Use your current job as your starting place. Make a list of the things you really like about your job. When you stop thinking, and complaining about the things you don't like, there is always a lot to be grateful for (go back and read the very opening to this book if you want a reminder). Keep in mind the positives and spend less time dwelling on what's wrong.

From here you could go on to achieve whatever it was you wanted to, providing you are willing to take responsibility for your own future and to take the actions required.

Everyone who has been successful at anything began without knowing how to do it.

In the book, Outliers, Malcolm Gladwell talks about people who have achieved mastery of their fields and become highly successful. He suggests that to master a skill or discipline requires 10,000 hours of practical application. David Beckham spent much of his childhood playing alone with a football, Bill Gates spent hours learning computer programming after school, and the Beatles spent years playing in German clubs for ten hours a day before they broke into the big time.

There is no short cut to mastery, but you can choose to start moving in that direction right now.

What would it take to truly master what you do? Perhaps you need to acquire new skills, broaden your experience, read more books, or ask more questions.

It is your choice to either invest your time in improving your skills and deepening your knowledge, or not. My overwhelming experience of people I have met has left me in no doubt that when you begin to invest in yourself, new doors open and things change.

We get paid for the value that we bring to the market. Our individual value is made up of our skills and attitude. As our skills develop and our attitude refines itself, we become more valuable to the market. This gives you better opportunities for advancement and improved lifestyle.

> *One of my managers wanted to give a pay rise to an employee in her team. He had some important knowledge and she was afraid of losing him. He had made noises that he was unhappy with his salary and was actively looking for an opportunity. The next time I visited the office I sat down with him. I told him how valued he was, but that also he earned the money he earned because that is what the company paid for people with these skills. I suggested that if he wanted to earn more money, he should be asking himself what he would need to learn to demonstrate that he was ready for a move to a bigger role. He had not had this explained to him previously and it changed his perspective.*
>
> *Within six months he gained promotion to a bigger role. He had learnt that he was paid for the skills and attitude he bought to the market.*

How far should I go?

One thing we can learn from trees is that, despite their limited lifestyle options, they know a thing or two about growth. A tree grows as high and as wide as it can, given the resources available to it. You should do the same. How far could you go if you did the extra learning, acquired the skills, and pushed yourself?

It depends again on what it is that you truly want, and what is an acceptable trade -off for you

One of my audit managers came to see me. He had a growing son and was finding it difficult to balance the demands of his job with his desire to contribute to his son's upbringing particularly as he had a one hour commute in each direction to his home (property was much cheaper where he lived). The culture of the company we worked for was high performance and since my arrival I had maintained the pressure to improve the productivity of the team. He was on a high salary with a company car, a huge benefits package, and a 25% performance bonus. I said to him that I was not in a position to influence his work/life balance.

The demands of his role had always been high, and would continue to be high. If the current balance was not working, he would have to make a trade-off and perhaps look to move nearer to work, or to think about looking for a role where the hours would be fewer. I did counsel him that he was unlikely to find a role that paid the type of package he was earning that wouldn't require the hours he had to put in.

Your company is not responsible for deciding what the right trade-off for you is. It's your life, and ultimately it is about what you want, but there are trade-offs to be made. Will you reach for the remote or the book?

I watched a documentary about Warren Buffett, the investor, and at one point the richest man on the planet. It's an intriguing story, because in spite of the fortune he accumulated, he remained living in the same house, driving the same car, and even eating at the same local restaurant as when he had no money. His business partner was interviewed and revealed that both of them did what they did because they loved the process of investing in companies. He even went on to say that if they had preferred watching chorus girls that the Hathaway Company would never have been created.

If you find something that you REALLY love doing, the trade-offs become easier to make and so does being successful, provided you are persistent.

"A journey of a thousand miles begins with a single step" Lao-Tzu

Wherever you are now, the start of a new direction is only one step away. Point yourself at what you really want, and move in that direction.

How do I show up?

I worked with a swimming pool builder. He is a brilliant businessman and a volatile character. He was passionate, driven, and ambitious. His customers loved him because they were just like him.

I came into his office one day and he was looking a bit red-faced. I knew that generally meant he'd had an argument with someone. Then I noticed there was a dent in the wall, so I put two and two together. I opened the session, "Out of interest Martin, why is there a dent in the wall?"

"I've just punched it." He replied.

Following a meeting with an employee he got so frustrated with him that as soon as the employee had left the room, he lost his cool and punched the wall.

I said, "Okay, take me through what happened." He told me about the mistake the employee had made. Then we talked about the outcome for the business. The outcome was that he now had a hefty repair bill for his wall, a bruised hand, and the same ineffective employee he had before the incident.

Then I said, "What if you had chosen a different response to this? What if you had gone with 'I am going to be okay with this'?"

There was still too much anger and he didn't buy into that. He said, "Yeah, but look at what he has done."

I said, "Can you think of a time in your life when something really bad has happened, and your response had been calm and a positive one, one that enabled you to see with clarity what you needed to do, and to be able to act on it?"

He nodded and confirmed that there had been times when he

169

was Mr Cool personified when under pressure.

We all react differently to events. In a crisis, some people panic, and others calmly try to fix the problem. This is quite natural, but the outcome of any situation is a function of how you react to it. It is useful to know, and easy to forget, that you are free to choose. In fact, you make these choices all the time without realizing.

When you wake up in the morning you can make the choice about how you will show up in the world. You can choose to operate from a place of control, or a place of reaction.

Control

Choosing control means that you take ownership of what happens during your day. You will control your attitude and the outcomes that you will get from the day.

Choosing control allows you to:

- Get important stuff done
- Calmly deal with 'on the day' challenges
- Keep a sense of perspective
- Go home with a sense of achievement

Reaction

Alternatively you can choose to react to events and then spend your day blaming them for your lack of progress.

Choosing reaction leads to:

- Constant reshuffling of priorities and lack of movement on your 'to-do' list
- Knee jerk reactions and quick fixes to problems
- The sense that you are a victim of events
- Getting home and wondering where the day went
- Stress and an early grave

In 2009, I visited a recruitment company. The recession was beginning to bite hard.

Recruitment companies typically suffer early on in recessions. In this case the two owners told me, "9/11 hit us hard and now this recession has. Our clients aren't recruiting. There is nothing we can do"

I asked them a question. "What would it take for you to grow your business profit by 50% in the next year?"

One of the partners gave me a look of bemusement. "It's impossible because our customers are not recruiting and the market is highly competitive, driving price erosion"

I assumed he misheard me and so I asked the question again. "What would it take to grow your profit by 50% in the next year?"

The two partners looked at each other and then at me. This time they looked a little pissed off, as though I hadn't been listening to them. They repeated, in unison, their previous statement. They even looked affectionately at each other, pleased that they were unified in their condemnation of my dumb question.

I sensed they were ready to throw me out so I said, "Okay, let me ask you the question one more time. What would it take to grow your profits by 50% in the next financial year?"

Finally, one of the partners said, "Well for a start we'd have to probably take a look at some markets we don't operate in, and perhaps a look to cut some of our costs,"

I said, "Okay, tell me about that." Before I knew it we had a conversation going and new ideas emerged about how they could grow their profits in the next year.

Ten minutes earlier there had been nothing they could do.

You have control of how you approach each day and what you choose to give attention and focus to. No one and nothing can piss you off without your permission, and you are free to choose your response to any event that occurs.

EVENT + RESPONSE = RESULT

Improving on perfection

> *I went for an interview with an Insurance and Risk Management company. Part of their standard recruitment process was an inbox test. You were given a bunch of papers, including memorandums, articles, and telephone message notes. In twenty minutes you were required to sort them into order of priority for how you would deal with them. I could not do it. My brain went like scrambled eggs and I just couldn't figure out a pattern to it at all. I never got the job and it troubled me for years.*

Have you ever noticed that when asked to list their own inventory of strengths and weaknesses people can fill a page of weaknesses but struggle to explain their strengths?

- Whenever I am presented with a spreadsheet of numbers to analyse, as soon as I look at it they seem to perform a dance on the page for me

- I have to take notes as I read, because I can't recall the details of things I read yesterday

- It is physically impossible for me to keep a desk tidy or to religiously follow a diary and task management system

I could probably fill this book with a stream of bullet points like this. I read books to help me, attended courses, and tried to model myself on people who were better at these things than me.

Then I just stopped bothering.

Just like a business has to make trade-offs, humans do as well. My DNA, upbringing, and whatever universal force went into shaping me, gave me some skills that I am rightfully proud of. These super powers came at a cost. The cost was that for every super power I got, there was another I didn't get given.

Do you think Spiderman should spend time trying to improve his ability to hold his breath underwater and swim like a fish? Why would he waste his days and his gifts with that futile exercise?

So to be the best and most authentic version of me, I now just focus on what I am good at. Guess what, it is a pretty big list too. But I also realized that my weaknesses were offset by my strengths. My super powers help me deal with the stuff I am not good at.

- Whenever I am presented with a spreadsheet of numbers to analyse, as soon as I look at it they seem to perform a dance on the page for me. **My ability to ask incisive questions and listen with nothing on my mind helps me get to the bottom of any issue without burying my head in numbers**

- I have to take notes as I read because I can't recall the details of things I read yesterday. **My ability to cut straight to the heart of an issue, side stepping the superfluous information, is born out of my inability to recall detail**

- It is physically impossible for me to keep a desk tidy or to religiously follow a diary and task management system. **My ability to spot talents in others enables me to find people who are good at organizing me, leaving me free to focus on what I do best**

Stop worrying about the skills and gifts you haven't got. Don't compare yourself to other people. Put all your energy into the skills you have got. Use what puts you in flow.

Shout about your strengths and your weaknesses. They are part of your grounding and part of who you truly are. You do not need to fix them.

I still invest thousands of pounds and hundreds of hours into my own development. I read, attend conferences, meet and interrogate interesting people, watch TED talks, but with one key difference, I FOCUS ON IMPROVING WHAT I AM GOOD AT, NOT TRYING TO MASTER WHAT OTHERS ARE BETTER AT.

Summary

"Be yourself. Everyone else is already taken" –
Oscar Wilde

Something inside of you knows what you want to do and be. If you get in touch with that, life becomes easy and taking action is effortless. Look inside yourself for the answers and spend less time looking outside for what you think you want.

Don't buy into your story and your thinking. See it for what it is, just a personal myth. When you do this, the right solutions and next steps for you become obvious. The path of least resistance will become clear.

You should not be frightened to pursue your happiness, and companies should not be afraid to lose employees who are not happy in their jobs, or with what the company does. There are plenty of other people out there who will be.

The grass isn't always greener on the other side (remember the Formula One mechanics). Taking the ungrounded you into a new situation will get you the same results. GO INSIDE YOURSELF FOR THE ANSWER.

NEXT STEPS FOR WAKING THE TIGER

If you are a business owner or an executive involved in running a business, you will be doing it for:

- money to fund a lifestyle or dream

- the love of business itself

- the love of what it is you specifically do in business

At some level, it doesn't matter why you have ended up doing what you do. In an ideal world it would be a blend of all three. What does matter is that you enjoy what you do and always show up ready to put your 'A' game on.

Working 80 hours a week in a state of overwhelm is not an 'A' game strategy, and nor is cruising along bored. The 'A' game shows up when you are excited, cracking on, having fun and not taking yourself so seriously.

So how do you show up ready to play at full tilt?

In this book I have outlined the four things that matter for business success:

1. having a solid grounding in the big picture of business that extends across the whole company, as well as a detailed understanding or your own functional expertise

2. getting things done in ways that make the most of the strengths you have and the type of person you are

3. the strength of the relationships you have with customers, suppliers, colleagues and employees

4. operating from a place of strong personal grounding and awareness of where your 'awesome' is

That is where I come in.

I help people arrange themselves in such a way that they get the results they want in business, easily and enjoyably. We start by stripping away all of the BS you have been telling yourself so you get back to the brilliance that you are. Then we add in a deeper understanding of how business works and how you work. You get baked for six months in this marinade until the best version of you emerges, instead of the version you have been trying, or pretending, to be.

As we progress this journey, the business results you seek will begin to arrive quicker than you could imagine from your current viewpoint, and in ways that are fun and effortless.

How I do it?

Initially we spend a day together figuring out where you are now and what is stopping you smashing through whatever self-imposed ceilings you have placed on your performance. From that place, we work on adding in what you need more of and subtracting what you don't need.

We will speak every week and meet every month, away from your place of work. In between sessions, I am there for you (email or phone) when you need me to support with difficult situations, discussing ideas and getting past obstacles. You will also have access to my "Everyday MBA" toolkit to help you deepen your knowledge of the whole picture of business.

At the end of our time working together you will have:

- a big step up in the results that are most important to you in your job or business

- bags of self-confidence that is grounded in an understanding of how you are at your very best

- deeper self-awareness of what your real strengths are and how to capitalise on them

- stronger relationships with the people you depend on for results

- more productivity and resources available to you

- a realisation that work has become effortless, enjoyable, and dare you say it, fun!

Of course you could do nothing and stay as you are - but this has a cost too. Every day you show up as the current 'best version' of yourself the results suffer and you suffer. Business is and should be fun, so why waste a day of your life deferring the results you seek?

Alternatively, you could invest in an MBA, a management development programme or employ a coach for a few years. All of these solutions will be more expensive, less fun and slower to deliver the results you really crave.

Your business or career is a vehicle for you to achieve what you want from life. This is far too important, and life is far too short, to play at anything other than full tilt. This programme equips you to do just that.

If you are a business owner or a decision-making executive, you can book a two-hour session to road test me without handing over a penny.

In this session, we will explore three things: what do you really want, what is stopping you, and how do you move forward. This session will rock your world and leave you buzzing

After those two hours are up, we'll have a few different decisions we can make together.

1. *"WOW! Dave you really did rock my world! How can I get more of this?"* - and we'll figure out the best way to work together in the structure I've laid out.

2. *"WOW! Dave this is great stuff, but I'm not sure I'm ready to jump in. Is there a way to ramp up to a full-blown relationship like the one you suggest?"* - and I'll help you figure out what we can do and on what time scale. Maybe it will just be some resources you can access on your own, maybe something more, but we'll figure that out together.

3. *"WOW! Dave this stuff rocks!!! You know what, it's not for me BUT I have someone who should definitely meet you. I'll set it up to spend the same kind of two hours with them."* - I will then take care of organising to meet them and give them the same quality of experience that you got.

4. *"Dave, thanks, but it's just not what I'm looking for right now"* - and that's okay too, who knows what the future holds for us both, but then we'll both know to a better extent where the possibilities are, and we'll leave having spent a bit of quality time together. I'm betting we will both be better off for it too.

So what is it going to be?

Book up the two-hour session at www.sleepingtiger.co.uk and let's find out!

APPENDIX 1 - THE BUSINESS SCOREBOARD

I remember watching an American Football game on TV during my first business trip to the States. It was all very colourful and occasionally quite exciting, but ultimately dull. My interest level deteriorated purely because I just couldn't keep up with what was going on. Statistics flashed over the screen and I couldn't navigate my way through them to even figure out who was winning. I switched off.

For business, the scoreboard is the accounts, so anyone who is interested in the performance of the company should have the ability to understand the accounts, at least at a basic level.

In other words, the only reason not to be interested in the numbers is if:

- You don't understand them
- You are not interested in the performance of the company

Accountants have built an industry around the complexity of accounting, all with the laudable goal of making the numbers more meaningful. By way of pay back, if you don't understand any of these ideas, go and sit with one of the finance people and let them explain it to you. Don't be afraid, they will love to see you. They don't get many visitors.

There are three principle financial reports that companies use to report their performance to their investors, shareholders, and the Inland Revenue:

Profit and Loss Account - The report shows the how much net profit the company made and how that was achieved

Balance Sheet - The balance sheet provides a view of what the company owns and what it owes

Cash Flow statement - This shows the movements and sources of cash coming in and out of the business

The report most managers head for first is the profit and loss account, whereas investors will make a beeline for the balance sheet. To understand a company fully, the three need to be used in conjunction with each other.

Before we look at the reports, there are a couple of general principles that are important to understand about financial reports.

- All financial reports are a 'snapshot' of performance taken at a moment in time

- Some of the numbers used are not real. There are many estimates and assumptions made by accountants when compiling these reports. These assumptions have to be disclosed for large companies in the notes that accompany their accounts. I will explain the key ones

- Large companies have their accounts audited by independent accountants to verify that they are a 'true and fair' view

- The numbers are only ever really valuable when there is something to compare them to, such as the company's targets, or the performance over the same period last year

One of the CFOs I worked for used to refer to some of the accounts in his balance sheet as 'jars of pixie dust'. If the profit and loss wasn't showing particularly strong trading, he would sprinkle the pixie dust to improve the results.

Profit and Loss - Did we win the game?

The profit and loss account is the scorecard for the game. It shows whether the company made a profit in the time period it shows. The key numbers are:

SALES - Sales is the value of sales the company made. This might be actual takings; orders received, or confirmed commitments, depending on the company's accounting policy.

COST OF SALES - Cost of sales (also sometimes called variable costs because they vary according to sales volumes) are the costs the company incurred to buy/manufacture the products they sold. For example, if a company makes cars the cost of sales will include the cost of the raw materials and components. Again, depending on accounting policy, the company may also include production costs (factory operating costs and assembly workers wages). Some companies also include some elements of their marketing costs, such as commissions and other direct acquisition costs.

GROSS PROFIT - Gross profit is the difference between the value of sales and the cost of sales. It is normally expressed as a value and as a percentage. The gross profit percentage will vary wildly depending on what the company sells.

OPERATING COSTS - Operating costs (sometimes referred to as fixed costs because they are incurred by the company, whether it sells anything or not) are the general expenses the company incurs, such as the costs of people (salaries, benefits, training), rent and rates, utilities (light, heat, and power), repair and maintenance, advertising and marketing costs.

NET PROFIT - Net profit is the value left after all of the fixed and variable costs. Again it is expressed as a value and as a percentage.

Some companies that have high initial investments to make when they start up, such as telecommunication companies, often use a slightly modified net profit figure **EBITDA - or Earnings before Interest, Tax, Depreciation, and Amortization.** As far as I can tell (and fully expecting to incur the wrath of accountants everywhere), this is just a way of adjusting for the impact of the funding of lots of capital assets, and showing the supposed true underlying profitability of the company.

BREAK EVEN - The Break Even point is the point at which a company is generating enough sales to cover all of its costs. It looks like this:

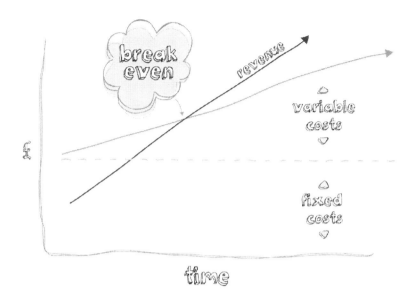

A business operating below its break-even point is in a loss making position, and will be in a cash-burn position.

> *The telecommunications start up I joined was funded by a group of private equity investors to the tune of $1bn. The rate of cash burn was astonishing, and although we scraped together a second round of funding, the company eventually wound up after simply running out of cash before it could get itself in position for an IPO (an offering of shares to the public to provide further funding). The company had missed the telecommunications stock explosion by a few years and the City had lost its appetite for tech stocks, otherwise I wouldn't be sat here writing this book, I would be sunning myself with a Pina Colada in my Californian beach condo.*
>
> *I was consoling my recently redundant self with a bunch of bankers who were in the same situation after quitting their jobs to join this exciting start up. In discussion with one of them, I mentioned that I felt I had wasted eighteen months of my life. He looked at me with surprise and then said, "Dave, if you haven't learnt anything from watching a business blow a $1bn*

in just a few years, then I really feel for you". He was right.
This experience taught me more about financial control than
any other.

NUMBER MASSAGES

Accountants have to make a number of assumptions or estimates in most profit and loss accounts. The two most important ones are:

BAD DEBT PROVISION - This is an allowance in the operating costs for customers not paying for the products and service

DEPRECIATION - This is an allowance made in operating costs to account for the fact that the assets that business uses are steadily losing value. Most companies have to buy capital items, e.g., machinery, plant equipment, and vehicles, which over the course of their useful life deteriorate in value. Depreciation is a way of spreading this loss of value rather than just taking a hit at the end of the assets life

MATCHING - It took me bloody ages to get my head around the accounting principle of matching, although it is actually so simple it defies belief. In order to make the gross profit figure actually mean something, it is important that the cost of sales in the period MATCH the sales of the period.

So, if I bought 50 tins of beans at £1 to sell in March, but I only sold 25 tins at £1.50, without using the matching principle, it would look like I made a loss:

Sales   37.50

Cost of Sales 50.00

Loss   (12.50)

But of course I still have 25 tins to sell. Let's say I sell them in the next month. Without using the matching principle, my Profit and Loss Account would look like this:

Sales   37.50

Cost of Sales   00.00

Profit   37.50

Using the matching principle will only take into account the cost of the actual goods sold, giving a truer picture of the businesses trading, so will look like this:

Sales   37.50

Cost of Sales   25.00   (only 25 of the 50 tins were used to make
the sales figure)

Profit   12.50

Of course not using the matching principle does not give an accurate reflection of my true trading. For the purposes of simplicity of bookkeeping, small businesses do not have to apply this matching principle. Whilst this certainly saves accounting fees, it makes their profit and loss accounts about as useful as an ashtray on a motorbike.

The Balance Sheet - what shape are we in?

In a rare moment of plain speaking, the balance sheet was named because it does exactly that, balances.

In order to understand a balance sheet there is a simple equation

CAPITAL + LIABILITIES = ASSETS

CAPITAL - This can be made up of money the owner or investors have put into the business in return for owning a share of the company.

LIABILITIES - These are the amounts the company owes to other organizations. These are split into:

- Long Term Liabilities, which include mortgages and bank loans

- Short Term Liabilities, which include money owed to suppliers, money paid by customers for services not yet delivered, and short term financing tools, such as overdrafts

ASSETS - This is the actual value of what the company owns. These are split into two/three categories

- Current Assets - these are assets that are, or can quickly be turned into cash and include cash in the bank, debtors (money owed by customers) and prepayments (payments made to suppliers in advance of them providing services)

- Fixed Assets - these are assets such as property, plant and machinery, and investments the company owns

- Intangible Assets - such as intellectual property in brands or designs, and goodwill (see below)

The balance sheet enables investors and other interested people to understand how the value of the company is made up and how it is funded. The balance sheet is also used in conjunction with trading performance to work out how much a company is worth.

The balance bit of balance sheet now makes perfect sense. A company can only have assets that are equal in value to the money that was either put into it originally, or has been lent to it.

A company's value is not based solely on the value of its assets. A company may only have a few fixed and current assets, but it may have an enviable customer base, access to a particular market, a great piece of intellectual property, or a strong relationship with some important suppliers. This may make it particularly attractive to a company looking to expand its own reach.

If company A has an asset value of £50m, and company B purchases it for £75m, the £25m difference is what is known as **GOODWILL.**

CASH FLOW STATEMENT

The cash flow statement for a company is used to show the movements in and out of the company and the sources of those flows. It is useful because it provides a strong indication of whether the company has sufficient funds to meet all of its commitments, and whether it is able to sustain itself without using external funding. It is very similar to a normal bank statement, except it categorizes cash flows in and out under three types of activity:

- **Operating activity** - Inflows will be from sales or interest receivable. Outflows will be supplier payments, payroll and interest

- **Investment activity** - Inflows will include cash from the sale of assets and loans from customers. Outflows will be purchases of assets or loans to suppliers

- **Financing activity** - Inflows will include cash from investors, shareholders, or lenders. Outflows will be dividends and repayments

ABOUT THE AUTHOR

Want to take the next step to better results?

Dave works with companies, teams and directors, managers or owners to transform their thinking about business and themselves. From inspirational talks, board and team facilitation, mentoring and his flagship product, the Six-Month Immersion Programme.

Immersion programme

Open to only forty people each year, this is a chance to work 1-1 with Dave to improve your business results.

This approach bypasses years of coaching and avoids complicated leadership jargon and models. It helps business leaders to raise their game, have more fun, become more commercially aware, and most importantly, it helps them find their true personal grounding; the ultimate point of power from which to operate.

If you think you might be interested in discussing how Dave might help you or your company, then you can make an appointment for a free consultation with Dave at www.sleepingtiger.co.uk or email his PA, sam@sleepingtiger.co.uk.

62367670R00110

Made in the USA
Middletown, DE
21 January 2018